THE BALANCE OF POWER IN EAST ASIA

THE BALANCE OF
POWER IN EAST ASIA

Edited by
Michael Leifer

St. Martin's Press   New York

First published in the United States of America in 1986

Printed in Hong Kong

Library of Congress Cataloging-in-publication Data
Main entry under title:
The Balance of power in East Asia.
Based on lectures delivered at the Royal United
Services Institute for Defence Studies.
Includes index.
1. East Asia—Strategic aspects—Addresses, essays,
lectures.   I. Leifer, Michael.   II. Royal United Services
Institute for Defence Studies.
UA830.B35   1986   355.03305   85–26186
ISBN 0–312–06588–4

Contents

Preface Michael Leifer   vii

Notes on the Contributors   ix

PART I   POWERS, PAST AND PRESENT

1 **Britain's Route to and from the Far East**
   Lord Beloff   3

2 **The United States in East Asia: China's Response**
   Jonathan Mirsky   16

3 **The United States in East Asia: Japan's Perspective**
   Ian Nish   30

4 **The Soviet Union in East Asia** *Gerald Segal*   44

PART II   REGIONAL POWERS AND REGIONAL
CONFLICTS

5 **China: An International Power?** *Brian Beedham*   61

6 **Japan's Foreign and Security Policies**
   Brigadier Kenneth Hunt   73

7 **Australia's Outlook on Asia** *Philip Towle*   84

8 **Indochina: An Arena of Conflict** *Sir John Addis*   97

9 **Korea's Changing Security Environment**
   Richard Sim   107

PART III   REGIONAL COOPERATION

10 **The Role and Paradox of ASEAN** *Michael Leifer*   119

11 **Trade and Asian Pacific Nations** *Louis Turner*   132

273156

PART IV   REGIONAL PROSPECTS

12 The Balance of Power and Regional Order
Michael Leifer   **143**

Index   155

Preface

This volume originated from a series of lectures on the general theme of 'Britain and the Far East in the 1980s' which was delivered at the Royal United Services Institute for Defence Studies. During the course of these lectures it became evident that a much larger subject had been encompassed than the original theme had suggested; that the perspective from the Greenwich meridian had been superseded by the perspective of those global and regional states which make up the balance of power in East Asia. In consequence, it was decided when considering revision of the lectures for publication to broaden the scope and the title of the undertaking to correspond with this wider perspective.

Nonetheless, it was deemed most appropriate to begin with Lord Beloff's original discussion of Britain's route to the Far East amended slightly to take account of its return journey by way of political and military disengagement. The balance of power in East Asia has long ceased to be a matter of practical British interest. It is so for both Superpowers if to differing degree and has remained for the United States despite its bitter experience in Indochina. To the extent that its abiding strategic concern is the management of its global adversary relationship with the Soviet Union, China and Japan are states of more than regional importance. Dr Jonathan Mirsky and Professor Ian Nish who spoke originally on the same occasion have rewritten and extended their contributions to deal in turn with Sino-American and Japanese–American relations. Dr Gerald Segal, in a specially commissioned essay, fills out the Superpower dimension by examining the range of Soviet interests and priorities in the region.

The regional perspective is considered next. Brian Beedham and Brigadier Kenneth Hunt look respectively at China and Japan as resident states, while the view from the rim is expounded in an analysis of Australia's outlook by Dr Philip Towle. Two regional conflicts are examined also; one active but contained in terms of the degree and nature of external involvement, another dormant but with greater potential for truly explosive eruption. It is a matter of the deepest regret that Sir John Addis died before the publication of this collection of essays. His original lecture on the conflict in Indochina stands the test of time for its quality of analysis. Richard Sim then assesses the condition of Korea in the context of its changing strategic significance.

The third section considers aspects of regional cooperation and includes chapters on the role of the Association of South-East Asian Nations (ASEAN) conceived of as a diplomatic community by the editor and on the evolving pattern of trade among Asian-Pacific states by Louis Turner. In conclusion the state of the balance of power in East Asia is reviewed in terms of the prospect for regional order taking into account the contending and convergent interests identified in the body of the volume.

In preparing the volume for publication a major burden of responsibility was borne initially by Jennifer Shaw which was then assumed by her successor at RUSI, Brian Holden Reid. I am indebted to them both.

MICHAEL LEIFER

Notes on the Contributors

Lord Beloff was formerly Gladstone Professor of Government at Oxford University and then Principal of the University College at Buckingham from 1974 until 1979. When Buckingham was awarded University status he was elected Rector. He is the author of many books including *The Foreign Policy of Soviet Russia* and *Imperial Sunset*.

Jonathan Mirsky is the China correspondent of the *Observer*.

Ian Nish is Professor of International History at the London School of Economics and Political Science. His most recent book is *The Origins of the Russo-Japanese War*.

Gerald Segal has taught at the Universities of Wales and Leicester and is currently Lecturer in Politics at the University of Bristol. His books include *Soviet Strategy towards Western Europe* (edited with Edwina Moreton), *Chinese Defence Policy* (edited with William T. Tow) and *Defending China*.

Brian Beedham is the Foreign Editor of *The Economist*.

Brigadier Kenneth Hunt was formerly Deputy Director of the International Institute of Strategic Studies. He is now Visiting Professor in International Relations at the University of Surrey and a Research Associate at the Research Institute for Peace and Security, Tokyo. He is joint editor of *Asian Security* and is currently a member of the RUSI Council.

Philip Towle took a PhD in war studies at King's College, London, and taught at the Australian National University, Canberra. He is currently a Defence Lecturer at Queens' College, Cambridge.

The late Sir John Addis was sometime British Ambassador in Beijing. He was also a Fellow of Wolfson College, Oxford.

Richard Sim has worked as Head of Research at the Institute for the Study of Conflict, and Senior Research Analyst at Control Risks Ltd, where he had special responsibility for East Asian affairs. He has published several research reports and has contributed the Korean entries to the *Annual Register* since 1980. He has also written for the *Annual of Power and Conflict*, the Hoover Institution's *Yearbook on International Communist Affairs*, the *Contemporary Review*, *Soviet Analyst* and the *Handelsblatt*.

Louis Turner is a Research Fellow at the Royal Institute for International Affairs. He is the author of *Oil Companies in the International System* and *Newly Industrialized Countries*, and is currently working on a study of European–Japanese technological cooperation.

Part I
Powers, Past and Present

1 Britain's Route to and from the Far East

LORD BELOFF

My purpose is not to impinge upon what other contributors may have to say about our interests in the Far East or their implications for defence policy but to try to set these questions in a wider framework both historically and geographically. These two perspectives are difficult to separate. History, as I have come to see it, is primarily the study of geography over time – the changing relations between human groups and the organisations they form with the physical environment of the planet.

What makes the subject particularly difficult is that one is constantly struck both by what seem to be extraordinary continuities of experience and habit – as when we talk of the immemorial East – and at the same time by the rapidity of change not only in the relationships between human groups but even within them. Britain's period of overseas expansion which began in the sixteenth century and ended only after World War I was largely the product of individual settlers, entrepreneurs and not to put too fine a point on it, bandits, with the State coming in often only reluctantly and self-effacingly to protect its nationals and their interests and, as it were, to tidy things up.

As a result, the English were seen as a nation of individual adventurers ruthless in the exploitation of their superior skills whether peaceful or warlike, indifferent to their impact upon peoples with whom they came into contact, and imbued with a sense of inborn superiority which might permit a degree of paternal care for those subjected to them or even an intense and scholarly interest in their native cultures but which precluded any serious and continuous process of symbiosis.

British expansion was carried out by individuals, some motiv-

3

ated by greed, a few by religion, and many having no serious motive at all. We see little sign of an attempt to implant British ways of doing things, and where we find in the successor states of the Empire the survival of British administrative or constitutional practices or the use of English as a *lingua franca*, it is not because the British nation and state has willed it so, but because the former subject peoples have wished to have these things along with the more material skills of their former rulers. This view of the English as a nation of haughty adventurers which provided the foreign stereotype of the Englishman from the days of Francis Drake to those of Colonel Lawrence has in the course of little more than a generation vanished so completely that it requires an effort of the historical imagination to remind ourselves of how things were only yesterday. For reasons which would take us deeply into our own domestic history we have become increasingly collectivist in our outlook, neither admiring the entrepreneurial virtues nor providing conditions for them to flourish. So far from exhibiting a sense of racial or cultural superiority, we lean over backwards to express our admiration for other races and other civilisations; our instinct when our interests are challenged is to appease the challenger. The foreign policy tenets of nineteenth-century dissent in both senses have become our orthodoxy.

It is, of course, easy to point to the reasons why this should be so and to admire the prudence of statesmen who do not venture beyond the boundaries dictated by our physical weakness. Our armed forces have been dwarfed by the advent of weapon technologies of which only Superpowers, as the jargon has it, can make full use. Our earlier priority in manufacturing has been overtaken, so that by a curious paradox the ability to manufacture cheaply by way of which we got into the Far East to a large extent no longer exists; while it is Far Eastern countries themselves which can now out-sell us in our own markets. Nevertheless, it can hardly be denied that the psychological change is more remarkable than the changes in physical circumstance. When coal was the basis of most forms of energy we made the most of our ample and accessible supplies; now that we have almost alone among major industrial countries our own resources in oil – today's major energy resource – we do not seem to be able to make use of it in the same way.

CYCLES OF DEVELOPMENT

It is sometimes argued that we should free ourselves of the tendency to look back into history for illumination because no age has ever known change at the present rate. I believe this to be an illusion. Of course, there has been an acceleration in the application of science to technology and in scientific discovery itself, but the permanent features of the human condition have not changed in the same fashion. The expectation of life has gone up in all countries, except possibly the very poorest, yet where it has gone up it has been very largely because of a decline in infant mortality – the expectation of life for an adult in terms at any rate of working years is not so different; we do not expect much of anyone beyond the psalmist's three score and ten. In other words, the accumulation of experience by individuals and generations and their application to solving problems of social organisation and of economics and politics is not very different from what it was centuries ago. It has often been the case that the building up of states and empires, the creation and development of new trading routes has been a very rapid affair; and so too has been the disappearance of established economic patterns and the power and influence that has gone along with them. Contemporaries have never fully been able to apprehend the long-term cycles of development which have dictated their fortunes; and I see no reason to suppose that we are any better at it now.

Some historical phenomena are, however, more durable than others, or have proved so far in the past. Two of these stand out. Actual settlement of land whether by overland migration into contiguous territories – as in the case of Russia and China or overseas as in the case of the British in North America or Australasia – endures in a way that patterns of trade and commercial empires do not. Secondly, there seems to be a very important sense in which the implantation of religious beliefs proves to be long lasting, and a major determinant of political allegiance. And this would seem to be true even where secular tendencies have weakened the hold of the religious institutions themselves. In Europe, the boundaries between Catholic and Orthodox and even the later division between Catholic and Protestant remain an important factor in any attempt at political explanation. Outside Europe, the boundaries between Islam and

Hinduism, Islam and Buddhism or between Buddhism and Confucianism are still of great significance. Whether the original conversions were through willing assent or submission to superior force does not seem to alter the case. What is essential is that it should reach down far into the social structure; otherwise as with the fate of Christian missionary activities over most of Asia, after centuries of effort the result is likely to be quite superficial and often evanescent.

Religion is not ever by any means the only sphere in which decisions have been made by the arbitrament of force. Nothing is more foolish than the current downgrading of the historical role of armed conflict or the threat of it. It is all very well to mock at history which is only one of kings and battles. But the battles decide who in the broadest sense shall be the kings. In one sense, the movement of settlers and the building up of networks of trade and finance are in their nature phenomena of long duration; yet often the direction that will be taken is decided by the arbitrament of a single campaign, sometimes, especially at sea, of a single battle. It is not surprising that those who fail to see this fact in history make grievous errors when it comes to advocating policies for their own time.

THE EAST, OR THE FAR WEST

In looking again at the extraordinary story of Britain's route to the East, all the elements I have mentioned come into consideration: the exploitation of industrial advance against countries less developed – in India, South-East Asia and China itself; and the outcome of conflict with competitors on the same general level of achievement; defeats at the hands of the Dutch giving them for three centuries the mastery of the spice islands; victories over the French leading to the creation of British India which was the heart of the whole business; victories over the Turks and their German allies creating what one historian has called 'Britain's moment in the Middle East' and finally defeat unmitigated at the hands of Japan – the fall of Singapore. The collapse of Britain's position in Asia was more rapid that its construction had been. The seventeenth century was a time of beginnings not all of them fruitful. The eighteenth century saw the foundations laid of the Indian Empire; the establishment of

British control in South-East Asia (except for Indochina) and
the penetration of the Chinese and Japanese markets was a
nineteenth-century extension largely of the Indian sphere, and
was made possible to a very great extent by Indian resources;
the confirmation of a Middle East bridge for the imperial routes
coinciding with the advent of air communications was, as we
have seen, the most recent phenomenon of all. At the same time
the external conditions altered at a different rhythm but no less
dramatically. Both the Dutch Empire which was the oldest and
the French Empire which was relatively new came to depend
upon British sea power as Japan emerged no longer as a country
to be penetrated by Western commerce and influence but as a
major maritime power in its own right with an alternative view
of how the organisation of Asia, at any rate east of the Indian
sub-continent, might be undertaken. The United States, early
in the field from the trading point of view but originally reluctant
to see this followed by political involvement, became heavily
embroiled with the acquisition of the Philippines – itself a by-
product of a conflict whose origins lay in the Caribbean. The
Germans tried in the Wilhelmine period to enter into the
competition for trade and development rights in China and for
island bases in the Pacific but lost their holdings as a result of
defeat in World War I.

Meanwhile, Australia and New Zealand had become important communities in the British Empire which although self-
governing had come to depend upon the protection of the
imperial lifelines and eventually guarantees of their own soil
which they were not populous enough to provide for themselves.

Thus, when the coastal enclaves and island possessions of the
European allies and the Americans were lost in World War II,
an outer ring maintained not for the most part by direct
reinforcement from Britain but by supplies across the Pacific
from the west coast of America, came into play as the basis for
the ultimate turning of the tide against Japan. So while we think
of the East as the scene of this part of Britain's history it now
makes more sense to see it as the Far West. And this brings us
back to the beginning since it was the search for a westabout
route to China that brought the first European explorers,
including the first English sailors, into Far Eastern waters.

Three other developments preceded the collapse of Britain's
imperial system. In the first place, the Russians coming overland

and from the north became neighbours of the Indian Empire or of its buffer states. The absorption of Afghanistan into the Soviet Empire may be justified and indeed made inevitable by ideology but it is in line with what has so far been the continuous southward pressure of Russian colonisation and influence over the centuries. It is, as George Curzon saw a century ago, something which it is hard for a maritime power with its resources thinly stretched to resist. If it comes to an end in the future it will be because the people needed to continue the expansion are no longer available. Maritime history depends on technology and seamanship; history on land depends on differential birthrates.

We can see how far this is the case if we consider the other features of the two centuries, the competition between the Russians and the Chinese for the settlement of North-East Asia, an area where the Chinese have both the advantages of proximity and better capacities for adaptation to the severe conditions of the region. Outer Mongolia is the Afghanistan of an earlier generation. But the buffers that Russia has created are only credible so long as Russia's technological lead in weaponry survives. At the beginning of this century, Russia and Japan vied for primacy in north-eastern China; today they are rivals again but because of the new post-Revolutionary strengthening of the Chinese state they can only operate as its partners, and here, for many reasons, Japan has the edge.

CHINA

The changed role of China is the second of the three main changes in the external environment and the one most difficult to assess or interpret. Over much of the rim of Asia, British trade was carried on in close partnership with the Chinese themselves as they came to settle in areas under British (or Dutch) control. The relationship extended to Hong Kong almost wholly settled from China and the so-called 'Treaty ports'. The Chinese state resented this penetration and was coerced into accepting it as well as Western and mainly British tutelage. Under the banner first of nationalism and then of communism the Chinese state reasserted its independence and began to climb the steep path towards industrial and military competitiveness. As such it appears to offer the same opportunities to those who know how to take advantage of its needs as it appeared to offer earlier generations of traders. But the competitiveness of an industrial West seeking markets and the inability of any Western country to exercise coercion means that the relationships are now such as the Chinese choose to make them. And these in turn are linked not to the profit motive of individual Chinese merchants but to the plans of a centrally administered economy.

A special interest has been attached to the continued role of Hong Kong as a highly successful capitalist economy on the border of China and owing much of its success to its utility to the Chinese as a window on the Western world. Although Britain has maintained a garrison there since it was recovered from the Japanese at the end of the war, its inability to withstand an attack from outside has always been admitted; the main duties of the military have been to help keep down the illegal immigration from the mainland. This movement has shown that Hong Kong despite its overdrawing and stretched facilities has offered a better prospect of making a decent living than Communist China. Even the Chinese genius for commercial activity and the people's skill and thrift have not been able to overcome the heavy handicaps of socialist doctrine.

It is now clear that British rule, which was always bound to become precarious once the new territories were returned under the treaty obligations, is going to be relinquished by 1997. Political and military control will disappear and we shall lose the reminder of the twists and turns of imperial history provided by the presence in Hong Kong of the Gurkhas from Nepal, itself a buffer state between the Indian and Chinese worlds.

Assurances have been given that Hong Kong will not be directly assimilated into the Chinese economic and social order but will be allowed some kind of special regime which will make it possible for its business activities to continue to China's own profit. It remains to be seen whether Chinese pragmatism can devise a mechanism not merely distinct on paper, but such as to give confidence to the people of Hong Kong and external investors that it will endure. It is not clear at the time of writing that the Chinese have fully grasped what is entailed in creating confidence of this kind. In any event, some outflow of goods and people is to be expected so that this part of Britain's Far Eastern saga has not yet reached its end.

THE RISE OF JAPAN

The third major change in circumstances upon which we need to dwell is the rise of Japan. Japan's present situation in the world is doubly extraordinary in that having lost the bid to build an 'East Asia co-prosperity sphere' by the use of military force, it is now with the assent and under the protection of its former adversaries doing just that by a combination of trade and technical assistance. It may well be that capitalism as the Japanese practise it is somewhat far removed from the Adam Smith–Milton Friedman model – but it remains the case that however one analyses it, Japan is closer to something we might call capitalism and to a pluralist political system than it is to socialism; hence its success. There is no historical reason to believe that the Japanese are more gifted than the Chinese – on the contrary much of their culture is derived from Chinese influences just as almost all their modern technology has always been derived from Western models – Japan not only saves, as is often pointed out, from its low expenditure on defence; it also saves the high costs of much of research and development.

Apart from the Hong Kong anomaly, soon to go, Britain has now no direct ruling role in Asia; her interests are those of the rest of the industrialised world, peace, security and the possibility of fruitful trade and investment. From the point of view of the route to the East, the British withdrawal from East of Suez was perhaps an inevitable consequence of the decision to allow successor states to take over in the Indian subcontinent. It is possible to argue that a different rationale could have developed for maintaining a presence in the Middle East section of the route; and indeed the British involvement in Oman suggests that this is the case. But there, as in the Far East, it looks as though Britain, like other European countries with economic interests in these areas, expects the United States to act as their guardian and as the provider of security. In the Far East, the endeavour to substitute American for British power goes back a long way, to the abrogation of the Anglo-Japanese alliance and to the Washington Treaties. The assumption that Britain could not be a major power in both the Mediterranean and the Far East while providing for the defence of its own islands which was the root of the policy of appeasement was shown in the last resort to be perfectly correct.

THE UNITED STATES

It has, however, not proved a substitution of like for like. Although the United States had its own interests in China and in Japan, it was not the centre of a maritime commercial empire in the sense in which this was true of Britain, and to a lesser extent of the Netherlands and France. And even when Asia became the main scene of the global rivalry between the United States and the Soviet Union as in the wars in Korea and Vietnam, the stakes from the American point of view were always limited. Where the American problems have resembled those of Britain in the past, it has been in the logistic implication of the situation of which recent events in Iran and Afghanistan are all too pertinent a reminder. Furthermore, there is the new factor of Soviet naval power which means that while Russia's overland thrust is the most powerful of its agents of expansion, it can now be supplemented from seaborne forces, and that it is now able to bring assistance to its friends even where no contiguous frontier exists. The ability of the Soviet Union to sustain Vietnam as a close and viable ally, and indeed to use Vietnamese expansionism as an agent of destabilisation in South-East Asia despite China's hostility would seem to provide proof of this new strategic factor in the situation.

What the United States has rightly been seeking throughout the post-war period and even more assiduously since the partial *rapprochement* with Beijing is a situation in which the countries of the East could themselves play the major role in the defence of their own security. Except for China they have so far proved unable to fulfil this desire though for different reasons. Japan has been chary of embarking upon a renewed attempt at becoming a great military power for fear of the impact upon her internal condition, and has felt that the Americans in their own interests are likely to afford her the protection she needs. Her diplomacy swings between China and Russia with both of whom she would prefer to retain good relations although Russia's retention of her northern islands makes a serious *rapprochement* with the Russians very improbable. In a somewhat similar position to Japan is Australia; much has been talked about Australia's Asian destiny and indeed with the decline of the British market for her staples, a more regional view of her economic prospects was natural. But, as in Japan, there are strong internal pressures against taking over any further responsibility for the common defence. India might have been expected to take over the role of the British Raj having inherited its basic geographical and material circumstances. It has not done so partly for ideological reasons and partly because of its preoccupation with Pakistan. In so far as Indian governments have been prepared to see the world in terms of power politics, they have seen issues that divide them from China as more important than any threat from Russia, and imperialism as personified by the United States rather than by the expanding Soviet colonial empire. As Afghanistan has shown, the most striking success of Soviet diplomacy, in which arms sales and ideological penetration of course play their part, has been the neutralisation of India.

INDIA

I do not think that the importance of this fact of neutralisation can be over-estimated. For it is made manifest in relation to four important issues. Three of these arise from the Soviet take-over and occupation of Afghanistan. There is to be only a 'political solution' for Afghanistan which is another way of saying that the Russians are to be allowed to stay in that country until they themselves are satisfied with the security of the regime they have installed. It has been made plain that all attempts to build up the strength of Pakistan as a counterweight to this Soviet presence will be treated as indicating hostility to India. And India leads vocal and persistent opposition to the strengthening of Western naval power in the Indian Ocean and in particular to the strengthening of the facilities at Diego Garcia. Yet without this presence there can be no effective reply to a Soviet threat to the Gulf should this materialise as the Iranian Revolution and the Iraq–Iran war have made more likely. In another area of tension, the Indian government also insists on a 'political settlement' for Kampuchea which means accepting the hegemony of Vietnam over the whole of Indochina with the threat which this poses to the ASEAN countries, and first and foremost to Thailand.

I am, of course, well aware that in pursuing these polices, the Indian government believes that it has India's interests at heart rather than those of the Soviet Union. It does not see itself as inheriting the British need to balance the Russian thrust southwards; it sees the long-term threat as coming rather from China, the rival Asian centre of power and influence and a country with which it has border disputes. It has also had its perpetual suspicions of Pakistan envenomed by its anxieties over the impact of Islamic revivalism upon its own Moslem citizens. Nevertheless, it is the policies themselves not the range of reasons that lie behind them that affect one's assessment of the situation. And it is not without significance that the most vocal critic of India's policies has been Lee Kuan Yew of Singapore, who has, shown himself very sensitive to any developments that could endanger the remarkable economic achievements of his country.

BRITISH INTERESTS TODAY

Britain's route to Asia still presents landmarks that remind one of past mercantile enterprise and naval power. Indeed with the changes in the strategic scene, some features of a quite remote past would seem to be acquiring new importance – the Cape route for instance as a fall-back from Suez – we cannot be indifferent to the future of Simonstown. There have, of course, been vast changes – direct rule has been limited sharply; the successor states are, however, largely through Commonwealth membership, still susceptible in many cases to British ideas even if reserving the right to reject them. British interests are still important almost throughout the countries of both the inner and outer ring. There are interests that are shared by these countries themselves particularly by those whose prosperity depends on the movement of commodities in the world economy and also by other Western industrialised countries and by Japan.

All these interests are threatened both by the possible incorporation of further countries within closed economies of the Soviet type, which would subordinate their economies to Soviet needs or reduce their productivity through the imposition of political for commercial considerations as has happened in Vietnam and Kampuchea, and also through the spread of violence and revolutionary turmoil. Political stability with the prospect this offers both local and external investment is a much greater factor in wealth creation than foreign 'aid'. But how this is to be preserved where it exists or achieved where it does not is something which cannot be dealt with through general formulae, when the countries one is thinking of range in location from the eastern Mediterranean to the China sea.

In so far as the problems are those of military defence, Britain's role must in most cases be that of an auxiliary or at best a partner in some wider effort. The problem is one of making sure that the contributions we do make are those which make the best use of our resources. The history of Britain's armed presence on the route to Asia and in Asia has been, like so much in the history of defence policy, the result of hasty decisions made to satisfy financial rather than strategical considerations. That is not to say that financial considerations should play no part in our thinking but only that proper weight should be given at all times to the economic and hence the financial consequences of not doing things. Would we for certain have had our present problems in the Gulf if we had not adopted the policy of nothing East of Suez? Have we not gained so far to an inordinate degree from the relatively minor input into the defence of Oman? Arms sales and assistance with training must both be subordinate to a general assessment of British interests and the means of their defence.

As I have said, British interests are to a large extent identical with those of our friends, particularly in Europe. It is, therefore, not unreasonable to expect them to play a part in their defence. But our past professions are a handicap when we try to persuade them of this fact. Having justified the 'East of Suez' withdrawal by the argument that oil and other material interests could be safeguarded wholly by non-military means, it is difficult now to argue powerfully to the contrary. We worry about being accused of militarism by so-called Third World countries which have no hesitation in using military force against each other when their own interests appear to be involved. Nor does the flagrant use of armed force by the Soviet Union create the hostile reaction in world opinion that we sometimes too confidently expect. The peoples of Asia have suffered more calamities through lack of British strength than through its use to excess.

To say that considerations of security should play a proper part when we examine Britain's and the West's relations with Asia is not to say that other considerations are unimportant. It is simply to utter the warning that while Britain's failings in the past would seem to have grown out of a certain arrogance and a certain insensitivity to the feelings of others, the danger today is primarily one of excessive sentimentality. Excessive humility is as dangerous as its opposite. Nor should we accept the dangerous sophistry that would have us believe that while stability may be an appropriate goal for the advanced trading nations to strive for, the poorer countries do not benefit from stability but only from change. For stability does not exclude change – change is indeed inevitable in all societies if not on the surface then deeper down. But some changes produce not greater prosperity but the contrary. The sufferers through war and revolution in Asia (as indeed in Africa and Latin America) have been the refugees – from Bangladesh, from Vietnam, from Kampuchea and from Afghanistan. And it is largely the Western countries who have been left to make the effort to reintegrate these people into new lives far from home. We should not accept lectures in international morality from regimes whose own subjects vote against them with their feet.

2   The United States in East Asia: China's Response

JONATHAN MIRSKY

When Ronald Reagan received a 21 gun salute in Beijing on 26 April 1984, it was the highest such honour the Chinese had accorded a foreigner since the end of the Cultural Revolution. Beijing further honoured the American President by providing him and his wife with a reproduction of a Ming dynasty bed in their suite in the walled and secluded *Diaoyutai*, the Fishing Platform of the Qing emperors, in which China lodges important State guests.

The following night, in the Great Hall of the People, Chinese community leaders, as they were described, listened to Mr Reagan praise God and free enterprise. His words were relayed in print back to the United States, but not by television. Parts of the President's speech had, in fact, been blacked out of what had been expected to be a live broadcast. Nor were the Chinese masses informed that, stopping over in Honolulu, Mr Reagan, on his way to China had revealed 'the real purpose of our trip': a hazily conceived but unmistakable partnership against the Russians. To underscore this point, Mr Reagan reminded his audience in Beijing that it was not US troops the Chinese faced along their borders, and it was not an American fighter which had brought down the Korean jetliner the previous year.

China's leaders dislike antagonistic public references to third powers during State visits, unless they make them themselves, and these remarks, too, were excised from Mr Reagan's televised speech. Publicly, the Chinese allowed the impression to become widespread that they had spoken sharply to Mr Reagan about the Superpowers – both of them – as a threat to world peace; they had made clear, too, Beijing's spokesman said, that

16

China enters no pacts with either Superpower.

But it became known that Chairman Deng Xiaoping had said to the American president, 'Your country is once again a great one', and that Party General-Secretary Hu Yaobang had assured Mr Reagan that the Chinese expected at least 40 years of good relations with the US. In the opinion of top White House officials, there now exists a friendly relationship between the two countries, but not an alliance. China, they state firmly, has made a fundamental decision to tilt towards the Americans, in the interests of modernisation. Although muted, its purpose was to ensure its defence against the USSR. The Chinese have accepted the American view, now two years old, that China must be seen as an important *regional* power, not as a global one which can be played like a card against the Russians.

Washington, these highly placed officials say, no longer believes that China can play a significant role in American global strategy. They recognise that it is a poor backward country; that the relationship between the two countries, although friendly, is ultimately a fragile one; and that inflated rhetoric, of the kind once common in the Carter years, must be avoided. China and the US, it is now clarified in Washington, are friendly, but non-aligned. In fact, the relationship is probably much closer than that, but the outward signs of strategic links are being kept minimal by both sides.

In any event, both sides got a good deal from the Reagan trip. For China, it was a significant coup to persuade the most anti-communist president since Nixon to visit Beijing and look friendly. At that point in his career as president, Mr Reagan had still to meet a high-ranking Russian. For him, the trip provided a chance to look statesmanlike on the Great Wall in an election year, and to say nothing that looked or sounded either soft on Communism or treacherous to Taiwan. In fact, although his trip annoyed Taiwan, Mr Reagan took the opportunity in Beijing to reaffirm his loyalty to the Nationalists. This did not cause much of a problem; the two sides, intent on cementing their relationship, agreed to disagree on the matter.

In the event, the Chinese received something solid. Just as after the Nixon visit, Beijing found itself back in the international community, seated at the UN and eventually in full diplomatic contact with the US, so from the new friendship with Ronald Reagan the Chinese have obtained promises of high-level non-lethal military technology, and Mr Reagan has made fewer aggressive speeches on the Taiwan question.

By January 1984, the clouds of gloom which had obscured the possibility of better relations between Beijing and Washington had already evaporated. Premier Zhao Ziyang had left Washington exuding euphoria. Only eight months before Beijing had cancelled cultural and sporting exchanges with the Americans and was threatening that worse could follow. The Chinese were furious over what they took to be American backsliding over the 17 August 1982 joint communiqué, in which the US had undertaken to limit and then end arms sales to Taiwan. Relations came near to freezing when China's woman tennis champion defected in California, an American scholar accused the Chinese of abortion atrocities, and an arcane wrangle broke out over millions of dollars' worth of imperial railway bonds.

But in mid-1983 neither Beijing nor Washington wanted a break. New understandings were being born. In the months before Premier Zhao finally landed in Washington, the Americans finally abandoned their last expectations that China might become a well-armed American hit-man on the Soviet eastern flank. China, for its part, began tuning down its public rage over Mr Reagan's continued support for Taiwan, in exchange for American help with the modernisation plans which are the cornerstone of Deng Xiaoping's policies.

President Reagan had come to grips with Chinese realities. In 1978, with his eye on the presidency, Ronald Reagan had pronounced firmly, 'It is absolutely untrue that I am going to Peking ... this country must not abandon its friends in Taiwan or weaken our mutual defense treaty with them.' What Mr Reagan was to encounter, as he moved through his first term, was a People's Republic whose foreign policies were a mixture of Maoist continuities and Dengist transformations. The tenets of this foreign policy are easy to identify.

THE TRIANGULAR RELATIONSHIP

Since 1949, the key element in China's position in the world has been its relations with the two Superpowers, each of which, at one time or another, has contemplated using nuclear weapons against the Chinese, and with each of whom the Chinese have considered a strategic alliance against the other. China, furthermore, continues to oppose more than limited *détente* between the Soviets and the Americans because it believes that such a development would lead to some sort of Third World partition, with China as one of the principal victims.

At present, the Chinese are eager to form an international coalition opposed to the USSR, even though the reasons for anti-Soviet feelings may vary from ally to ally. Moreover, China is determined, sooner or later, to recover Taiwan. It has also recognised that it is not able to do so by force.

Finally, Beijing's leaders constantly affirm their country's autonomy and independence, and its position as a champion of the Third World, with no intention of tying itself to either of the Superpowers. Nonetheless, as Premier Zhao observed during his trip to Washington in early 1984, China distinguished between the US and the USSR. With the former it looks forward to deepening friendship – although not an alliance – while with the latter it hopes for normalisation and little more.

What is new in Chinese foreign policy since the 1972 Nixon visit, and more markedly after Mao's death in 1976, is what China, somewhat ironically perhaps, calls the Open Door. This policy has allowed an unprecedented degree of foreign penetration into Chinese life, often to a degree alarming to the Party which is ever on guard against what it refers to as 'spiritual pollution'.

Behind the Open Door and the historical continuities lie other constants: Beijing's conviction that Soviet power is growing, although at any moment, such as the Afghanistan invasion or Vietnam's bog-down in Kampuchea, it may encounter road-blocks. Beijing believes, too, that American global influence has been on the wane since the Vietnamese war began to go sour in the late 1960s – although under Reagan, the Chinese note, US determination to stand up to the Russians is increasing.

Waiting for American enmity to abate was a great mark of Chinese patience. Through most of the 1950s Beijing had been in close alliance with the USSR – following a brief moment in the mid-1940s when Mao, before he came to power, expressed interest in better relations with the Americans. The American response had been cold. Later, more delicate Chinese feelers were rebuffed, by John Foster Dulles. As the American defeat in Vietnam became more certain, Beijing began to notice signs of thaw in Washington's attitude towards the People's Republic of China. The 1972 Nixon visit, therefore, and more particularly the Shanghai Communiqué, a joint declaration by China and the US, were momentous victories. The Americans acknowledged the Chinese position that there is only one China and that Taiwan is part of that whole. The Americans undertook, as well, to reduce their forces in Taiwan and hoped for a peaceful resolution of the reunification issue. The following year, liaison offices were established in Washington and Beijing.

From 1974, the pace of movement towards full normalisation slowed. Watergate in the US, and in China the deaths of Zhou Enlai and then Mao Zedong made it difficult for either country to see clearly the next steps; even trade diminished. With the election of Jimmy Carter to the presidency the pace towards normalisation quickened. It was announced in December 1978, and formalised in January 1979, with full diplomatic relations, exchanges of ambassadors, and a US announcement that it intended to sever formal relations with Taiwan, although trade and cultural links would continue.

With Deng Xiaoping touring the US in the January after the normalisation, relations appeared to have struck a new high. In February, however, Washington surprised the Chinese by publicly disapproving of their invasion of Vietnam. Although in March the US agreed to release Chinese assets frozen for 30 years, by April the Chinese were angered when the Congress passed and Jimmy Carter signed the Taiwan Relations Act, committing the US to its defence. In December, however, the US Supreme Court held it legal for the Government to sever the mutual security agreements with Taiwan, and by January 1980, Defense Secretary Harold Brown had travelled to Beijing for what appeared to be the beginnings of talks on a mutual strategy.

'I look forward,' Brown said, 'to an increasingly close relationship between the American military and the Chinese military. We intend to take parallel action.' Brown seemed to be paving the way for the US to supply China with non-lethal military equipment, and the Chinese were expected to place millions of dollars' worth of orders.

ARMS SALES TO CHINA

'China is no longer an adversary,' said a policy-making official in Washington. Denying that the US intended blatantly to play off the Chinese against the Russians, he did concede that 'We'll probably evolve towards some sort of security relationship with Peking.' Sometimes this was put even more robustly. Zbigniew Brzezinski, the White House national security adviser, was quoted by a CIA official. 'If we can cosy up to Peking we can infuriate the Russians, and anything that makes them angry is good policy.'

That statement of intent appeared to mean that the US was considering selling certain items from a list once closed to China, such as helicopters, pilot-training equipment, and radar systems, equipment sometimes called 'dual use', but arousing retired Secretary of State Dean Rusk to say, when shown the list, 'That looks like a military list to me.' A State Department senior official said, 'It's making the Russians wonder what China would do if the West and the Russians went to war. Or, what we would do if the Soviets went after the PRC. It makes decision-making more complex in Moscow, and limits their ability to take risks. Look at their deployment of nuclear weapons. Now they target more of them on China, and less of them on us.'

But the approach of Ronald Reagan to the White House shook the foundations of the rapidly warming Sino-American relationship. In April 1980, candidate Reagan declared 'I would not pretend, as Carter does, that the relationship we have with Taiwan, enacted by our Congress, is not official,' and said further that he would not permit 'any foreign power', that is, China, to interfere with the law – which stipulated a commitment to Taiwan.

The Chinese responded bluntly. By the late spring of 1980, the *People's Daily* was carrying commentaries charging Mr Reagan with 'turning back the clock in Sino-US relations by attempting a revival of the "two Chinas policy".' 'The Reagan view,' Beijing insisted, 'ran counter to the 1978 joint communiqué in which Washington and Beijing had established diplomatic relations, and the US undertook to close its Taipei embassy, remove its troops, and dissolve the mutual security agreement with the Nationalists.' It was no good, Beijing warned, attempting to establish an even-handed relationship with Taiwan and the mainland. This would resemble tightrope walking 'between good and bad ... between aggressor and victim'.

Nonetheless, the new administration announced in January

1981 that it was considering upgrading relations with Taiwan. Soon thereafter, China reduced its diplomatic links with the Netherlands, supposedly for agreeing to supply submarines to Taiwan, but actually as a clear signal to the US. Taiwan had emerged once again as the bone of contention between the two countries.

At the core of the dispute lay the words 'recognise' and 'acknowledge'. Beijing's position was clear: 'One of the important principles governing the normalisation of Sino-American relations is that the US recognises that there is only one China and that Taiwan is a part of China.' In the 1978 communiqué it had been stated that the US 'recognises' Beijing as the legal government of China, and that it 'acknowledges' China as one whole, governed by Beijing, with Taiwan under the same jurisdiction. Washington policy-makers pointed out that the two words were rendered by the same Chinese word as 'to take as a fact'. One highly placed source admitted that the hope of the Carter administration had been 'interpret this anyway you like'.

When Ronald Reagan met Premier Zhao Ziyang at the May 1981 summit in Cancun, and his Secretary of State soon thereafter travelled to Beijing, the administration began to fully understand the importance of Taiwan in Chinese thoughts. Secretary Haig's views on the Soviet Union were welcomed by Chinese leaders, as were his revelations that the US intended to sell lethal weapons to China – although it emerged later that Chinese thinking was changing on a strategic relationship with the Americans, which had begun to look very expensive. Indeed, Haig gave Beijing the impression that the US had in mind a subservient role for China in the strategic triangle with the Russians. China took this intention as an inducement to abandon its determination to resume control over Taiwan. When this Haig message was followed by Mr Reagan's disclosures from Washington that the CIA had established a station in Chinese central Asia for observing Russian rocket launchings, the embarrassed and enraged Chinese gave Haig a bleak airport farewell.

Within hours of Haig's unceremonious departure from Beijing, the Chinese released their terms for negotiations with the Soviet Union. The Chinese were making plain their unwillingness to be played as an anti-Soviet card in the American hand. Beijing was also 'waving away the illusion that it would swallow the bitter pill of arms sales to Taiwan', especially if this was to be balanced by similar sales to the mainland. Shrugging off the inducement, the Chinese said, 'These arms are not at all sophisticated. If they were, they would not sell them to others.' The Chinese also reminded Washington that in the past they had given up Russian aid rather than yield to Soviet bullying.

In the spring of 1981 a new American policy had developed: to permit arms sales to both the PRC and to Taiwan. But nothing significant had been shipped to the mainland while Taiwan continued to receive all but the latest fighters and other advanced material. Although the National Security Council had in principle approved a case-by-case sale of arms to Beijing, no deals had actually been signed, and on 18 June, the official Chinese news service was threatening that relations were worsening. Indeed, one interpretation of Beijing's earlier offer of terms to Taiwan was that it was a prelude to some sort of downgrading with the Americans.

Alarm at such a prospect was sufficient in January 1982, for Assistant Secretary of State John Holdridge to fly to Beijing to assure the Chinese leaders that the US would not sell Taiwan its most up-to-date fighters. On the tenth anniversary of the Shanghai communiqué President Reagan dispatched letters to the main Chinese leaders who wrote back. Both sides expressed hopes for better relations.

In May, Vice-President Bush travelled to Beijing to discuss once again the Taiwan arms sales issue and to prepare the way for the 17 August joint communiqué in which the US would promise to phase out slowly arms sales to the Nationalists, and in the meantime not sell them better ones. For their part, the Chinese agreed to refer to the American link to Taiwan as 'a question rooted in history', a formula periodically employed by China when it no longer wishes to confront a long-term problem in foreign relations, although the question remains open. On 29 October, Foreign Minister Huang Hua said in Washington that the relations between the two countries must be seen in 'strategic perspective'. Before long, however, Beijing newspapers were attacking American newspapers for referring to the commitment to Taiwan, and China cancelled a visit by its Chief of Staff, who had been expected in Washington to discuss arms sales. On 12 December, Deng Xiaoping told a group of Italian newsmen that both the US and the USSR were 'hegemonists'.

THE IMPROVEMENT OF US–CHINA RELATIONS

In retrospect, White House officials maintain that by mid-1982 the Chinese had already been reassured about the nature of American policy in general terms. In March, they pointed out, Defense Secretary Weinberger, speaking in Tokyo, had outlined what he termed the Six Pillars of American Asian policy. These included a long-standing friendly, but non-aligned China relationship, and a key global role for Japan, not China. No mention was made of an anti-Soviet triangle, with the US and China facing the Russian side. 'China appreciated all that', one official said.

Nonetheless, the first months of 1983 were a time of seeming crisis between the two countries. Small incidents, involving defections, irritations with students, and extraordinary disputes about Qing dynasty railway bonds became matters of state. But beneath the ferment lay an American determination to prevent things from getting worse and, if possible, to reach some basic understandings. The Chinese, too, it began to emerge, did not want a complete break with Washington.

In early February, Secretary of State Schultz arrived in Beijing, where Foreign Minister Wu Xueqian told him 'dark clouds' were hovering over the relationship. Letters from the parents of defecting woman tennis star, Hu Na, were placed in Schultz's lap. Hu Na had asked for asylum the previous year while competing in California. Eight months later, at a press conference stage-managed by a lawyer with close links to Taiwan, Hu claimed she had defected to avoid joining the Communist Party. The State Department's China desk, aware of mounting Chinese irritation with the United States, advised that Hu be returned to her own country. Immigration officials wanted her to remain. Although by the time Hu claimed asylum, perhaps a tenth of the Chinese studying in the US had indicated one way or another that they intended to stay, what enraged Beijing about the Hu Na matter was the tremendous publicity involved and an apparent Taiwan connection. When President Reagan eventually decided that he would be personally prepared to adopt Hu Na, Chinese anger overflowed, and a limited range of cultural and sporting arrangements were severed, although the bilateral educational exchange was not disturbed.

During the same period, an American post-graduate student,

Stephen Mosher, was dismissed from Stanford University for 'unethical behaviour'. Although Mosher's university denied that Chinese pressure had encouraged the drastic action, there was no doubt that Beijing had demanded strong measures against this student for publishing details of officially enforced abortion among women in rural south China. Mosher insisted that he had done little but report the facts, although he admitted that he had been unwise to publish his report initially, and anonymously, in a Taiwan-based magazine, including in it identifiable photographs of Guangdong women undergoing abortion. He subsequently published the same materials in a reputable US journal. Beijing accused Mosher of theft, smuggling, and other crimes, and suggested that the entire educational exchange had been endangered. For at least two years thereafter, no American social scientists were permitted to undertake extensive field research in the Chinese countryside.

Most peculiar of the bilateral disputes was the question of the Hu Guang railway bonds. At one point in mid-1983 Beijing was threatening to 'take appropriate action' if the US government seized twenty-six million dollars' worth of Chinese property to comply with a judgment against the PRC in an Alabama Federal Court. An Alabama electrical engineer, together with eight partners, had purchased bonds on the open market and were now demanding interest on an obligation incurred by the Qing in 1911, a few months before the dynasty had collapsed.

The bonds had been issued to pay for a railway which, the plaintiffs insisted, the Chinese State had used for decades. During the Schultz visit, Foreign Minister Wu handed the Secretary of State an *aide mémoire*: 'The so-called Hu Guang railway bonds were one of the means by which the traitorous Qing government, in collusion with the imperialist powers ... intensified its opposition and plunder of the Chinese people .... It stands to reason that the Chinese government refuses to recognise such old external debts.' The Chinese found it difficult to believe that the White House could not overturn the decision of the Alabama Federal Court ordering the Chinese authorities to appear before an American bench. Even though many legal experts were certain that China could not lose, the Chinese feared that appearing in Alabama might infringe their sovereignty.

The final obstacle to better relations was technology transfer. Although Deng Xiaoping and his comrades may have smarted each time President Reagan referred to 'our friends in Taiwan', sometimes even using the word 'government' for the Taipei authorities, Chinese leaders were above all dedicated to modernising the mainland. Just before Secretary Schultz took off for Beijing, the President, according to Washington officials, instructed him 'to look Deng Xiaoping right in the eye and tell him we want to be his friend'. Schultz delivered this message. Deng is said to have rejoined, 'Then why do you treat us like Russians when we try to buy your technology?' Deng had in mind Jimmy Carter's promise to him in Washington in 1979: China could have the latest advanced electronics, including computers. But the Pentagon had subsequently blocked delivery on the grounds that the items could have military application, and that in such matters the Chinese were always treated like Russians.

Schultz returned from the PRC determined to improve the relationship. On 5 March in San Francisco he delivered a speech putting an end to the notion of an anti-Soviet US–China coalition. The Schultz speech, like the one delivered the previous year in Tokyo by Caspar Weinberger, took an Asian overview perceiving China as a power important to the region, but not to the globe. It was Japan, Schultz made clear, that had assumed a global role. Not until China was fully modernised – which would be a long time coming – could it assume a position of international strategic importance. Nor, Schultz believed, did modernisation mean an up-to-date military machine. The Schultz team understood that China recognised a unity of interest with the Americans on Vietnam, Afghanistan, and Kampuchea, while disagreeing, naturally, over Taiwan, the Middle East and Central America. Schultz realised that the PRC no longer believed itself to be under direct threat from a USSR entangled in Afghanistan and over-extended by supporting the Vietnamese in Kampuchea. China now wished to be seen as an uncommitted Third World champion. The Schultz overview was a dramatic departure from the Haig vision of two years before, when Beijing was invited into a strategic alliance with the Americans.

Nor was it only the Republican hierarchy that realised that something had to be done to salvage Beijing–Washington good relations. In the late spring of 1983, Congressional Speaker Thomas 'Tip' O'Neill returned from China where he had undergone a top-level wigging from China's leaders on the subject of Taiwan and technology transfers. During a two-hour harangue from National Peoples' Congress Vice-Chairman Peng Zhen, said a witness, 'Peng sat on the edge of his seat and turned purple. We thought they had a lot of things on their minds, but everything came back to Taiwan.' But Deng Xiaoping and other leaders also raised the issue of technology. Upon his return to Washington, O'Neill recommended that 'bureaucratic obstacles need to be eliminated and the technology transfer process accelerated dramatically.' This sentiment was echoed by ex-President Richard Nixon, whom the Chinese regard as 'an old friend' as he prepared for his own trip to the PRC in early June. 'China should be treated the same as any other friendly, non-aligned country, like India,' Nixon advised. 'It is time to remove US agencies from the straitjacket which requires them to treat China like an adversary.'

It had already been done. During his visit in late May 1983 to Beijing, Secretary of Commerce Malcolm Baldridge guaranteed that all Chinese requests for technology would be expedited. Premier Zhao Ziyang's delighted response was deeply symbolic: the Hu Na matter was now closed.

In December, Secretary of Defense Weinberger was informed in Beijing that in January Premier Zhao would travel to Washington. The Weinberger visit was notable, too, for the low-key nature of the public statements about Sino-American military sales; this continued the modest tone set by the Schultz speech of March. The Chinese were now convinced that American thinking had changed: Taiwan would not be formally recognised, modernisation of the mainland had become an American priority, and China no longer figured largely in American military strategy against the USSR.

The Chinese set great store, they repeatedly state, on deeds rather than words. They had in fact been pleased by the wording of the 17 August 1982 joint communiqué promising an American phasing-out of support for Taiwan, and had been further reassured by the summer's agreements on technology sales (although by the following year, the summer of 1984, little if anything substantial had found its way across the Pacific).

The Zhao visit of January further cemented the relationship, as did the Reagan trip to China in April, which resulted in next to nothing in the way of agreements (except for an incomplete one on nuclear materials) but further demonstrated to the world –

and especially the Russians – the angle of the Chinese tilt towards the US. By late June 1984 the realities became still clearer. Defense Minister Zhang Aiping's semi-secret tour of American military installations culminated in the PRC becoming only the second Communist country, after Yugoslavia, to become eligible for US arms sales. The Chinese were promised avionics and jet training; in exchange Beijing agreed to sell the Americans a half-squadron of Chinese-built MiG 21s, at 4 million dollars each, to permit American pilots the experience of flying against Soviet-designed aircraft, even if the model was 20 years out-of-date. Agreements were also reached in principle for the Americans to sell China anti-tank and anti-aircraft weapons. Zhang, keen to maintain China's reputation for non-alignment, insisted that the contracts be kept secret.

Within a week or two of Zhang's trip, however, the nuclear deal, cobbled together so quickly in April to give Mr Reagan a signable document in Beijing began to come apart. It had been the culmination of three years' of negotiations. In Beijing the President's spokesman had claimed it met the American requirements for agreements with nuclear weapons states. But concern increased in the Congress, upon Mr Reagan's return, when the White House refused to allow inspection of the document, on the grounds that certain oral pledges by Premier Zhao, during his January visit, had been guarantee enough of non-proliferation. The US nuclear industry, in some despair, because of the recession and political opposition to nuclear energy, was agitating for a quick final agreement, so that reactors could be packed off to China in what would be a multi-billion dollar deal. Suspicions were now rife in the Congress that China was sending fissionable materials to Pakistan. Because the agreement had already been initialled in Beijing it could not be varied. Before long, China was accusing the US, once again, of backsliding.

But the basic Chinese position could be summed up in what Deng Xiaoping had told Mr Reagan in April: 'We agree with what you are doing in the Pacific'. The Americans know that the PRC has tilted in their direction. Both sides share a belief in Japanese primacy in the Pacific. The US has placed China in Category Five for technology transfers; NATO and Japan are also in Category Five.

President Reagan and Chairman Deng are pragmatists, willing

temporarily to abandon principle for medium-term gain. The President's heart goes out to Taiwan. But getting on with China, it has been explained to him, is economically and to some extent strategically important. In election year 1984 it also made statesmanlike good sense. Chairman Deng, for his part, seeks modernisation above nearly all else, and some anti-Soviet insurance, although this is not immediately vital. He also wishes to appear like a Third World leader. The Americans can accommodate this by not seeming to play a China card, while seeking to sell China as much as possible within the limits of its foreign exchange holdings – which are considerable. The White House claims that despite Chinese desires for the latest and best, it limits arms sales to the PRC in order to allay Soviet fears that an East–West vice is tightening on its borders.

The historic ironies in the relationship are enormous: the world's largest communist power is now counting for much of its modernisation on the world's largest capitalist power – which for more than 20 years alternately ignored and attempted to crush the Maoist revolution. Now that that revolution has been put into neutral, if not reverse, a devoutly anti-communist and pro-Taiwan American president is prepared to help modernise Deng Xiaoping's China. It is painful also to recall that more than 50,000 Americans and many hundreds of thousands, if not several million, Vietnamese, Cambodians, and Laotians died because a succession of American administrations, Democratic and Republican, underrated Chinese poverty and misunderstood Beijing's design and role in South-East Asia. Now Washington and Beijing, joined in hostility to Vietnam and support for the Khmer Rouge, are self-proclaimed 'friends' and despite claims to the contrary have moved into alignment.

3 The United States in East Asia: Japan's Perspective

IAN NISH

Both Japan and the United States had a change of housekeeper during the 1980s. In Japan, Suzuki Zenkō became Prime Minister and assumed the major task, faced by all postwar Japanese leaders, of making peace with the American president of the day. It was significant, therefore, that at the end of 1980, an American president was elected from the right wing of the Republican party. How would he with his new approach to national and international problems view the challenges presented by America's ally, Japan?

In Japan the general election of June 1980 had produced another in the long line of postwar victories for the Liberal Democratic party. On this occasion it secured 284 seats over the combined opposition of 227. This result reversed the trend which many observers had noted during the 1970s whereby the opposition parties were gradually inching their way towards assuming power, if they had been able to form and sustain an effective electoral coalition. Instead, the elections gave the LDP a secure position, leaving the conservatives stronger politically than they had been since the middle 1960s.

In place of Ōhira Masayoshi, who had died during the election campaign, the Liberal Democratic Party chose a new leader in Suzuki Zenkō. The choice was made for reasons of domestic politics, partly as a result of the strength of Suzuki's own faction and partly because of a compromise between faction leaders. He was not widely known in Japan itself, far less in the world at large. Nor had he any great enthusiasm for world affairs. He did not make a major overseas tour until he visited President Reagan in May 1981, almost a year after coming to power. Indeed he

30

had broken with tradition by undertaking prior visits to ASEAN countries.

The policy of the Reagan administration towards Japan differed from that of President Carter in degree rather than substance. It reiterated the need for the continuance of the American-Japanese Security Treaty. But because of its stronger anti-communist emphasis, it expected Japan to play a greater part on the military side. That being the case, it is appropriate that we should look back on some aspects of American-Japanese relations in the 1970s. These are defined by the Treaty of Mutual Cooperation and Security, signed on 19 January 1960 to replace the Security Treaty of September 1951. (By a paradox the Japanese still refer to the 1960 Treaty by the name given to the former 1951 Treaty.) The agreement – which is, after all, equivalent to an alliance commitment – states that each party recognises that an armed attack against either party in East Asia would be dangerous to its own peace and safety and that both would act to meet the common danger in accordance with constitutional provisions and processes. It seems that this formula is a comparatively weak form of commitment, all the more so because the treaty may be terminated on one year's notice on either side.

The relationship between the two countries has tended to be worked out in the past most prominently during annual meetings between the American President and the Japanese Prime Minister. Perhaps the most important of these meetings was that held in November 1969 between President Nixon and the then Japanese Prime Minister, Satō Eisaku. It was important because it was on that occasion that the United States promised to retrocede to Japan the Ryūkyū island group, which it had occupied since the end of the war. It came also at a time when Japan's economic miracle had begun to take effect and Japan had accumulated large trade balances, mainly at the expense of the United States. It was during these conversations that President Nixon, having offered the return of the Ryūkyū Islands, reportedly asked the Japanese cabinet to take into account the pleas of the American synthetic textile lobby against Japanese imports into the United States. Satō replied with an extremely polite expression which conveyed to the Americans the impression that he would take the appropriate action. When, in the months that followed, appropriate action did not seem to have been taken, the Americans felt that they had been substantially let down during this summit meeting. While communication is never perfect between nations, there are rather special hazards involved in communicating with the Japanese.

By the 1970s, Japanese growth under the shadow of the dollar had been spectacular. Japan's GNP grew second only to the United States in the free world and Japan emerged as a major competitor of the United States itself. It suddenly came to be criticised for over-exporting; and this was compounded, it was alleged, by the failure to give substantial foreign aid to developing countries and to make adequate outlay on defence. Amid a flurry of mutual criticism there took place a sort of minor trade war in which the United States retaliated against Japan. Congress first introduced quota legislation on synthetic textiles which was aimed against Japan and would have passed if it had not been overtaken in a tight legislative programme. In August 1971 the Nixon administration followed this by the famous import surcharge. After many months of hard bargaining the two reached an agreement in October whereby the Japanese would voluntarily restrain sales of synthetic textiles to the United States; the prototype for many later agreements for restraint. For the rest of the 1970s complaints arose from the United States' side over the export of a different range of goods: steel, colour television sets and cars. Perhaps the major breakthrough in economic relations came in 1978, when the Carter administration, supported by the United Auto Workers Union, asked that in order to overcome the major bilateral problem – namely, unemployment caused in the United States – Toyota and Nissan (Datsun) should open manufacturing, and not just assembly, plants in the United States. This was by no means an elementary decision for the Japanese to make. Japanese commentators knew full well that it might be unwise for them to build plants in the United States just when General Motors was moving its own production base abroad.

The second action of President Nixon which cast its shadow over American–Japanese relations in the 1970s was the clandestine American approach to the People's Republic of China in 1971. This involved a serious failure of consultation on the American side and, as some would say, a lack of imagination on the Japanese side. Many claimed that 'the American–Japanese alliance' had been breached unilaterally by Washington. While

Japan recovered her poise when Prime Minister Tanaka followed Nixon to Beijing in 1972 and succeeded in 'normalising' relations with the Chinese, the nature of Japan's special relationship with Washington was irretrievably altered. Of course, alliances have to be flexibly interpreted and have to be altered from time to time. It was inevitable that a security treaty which had originally been concluded in 1951 and revised in 1960 should be out of line with thinking in the 1970s. Prepared at a time when Japan's world interest was localised in the west Pacific, it had to be adjusted to take account of Nixon's Guam doctrine (1969) which, in the context of the Vietnam War, had given notice that the United States was disinclined to be so heavily involved in the west Pacific in future and looked to her regional partners to assume an increasing burden and role in their own defence.

The American failure to consult Japan in advance over the New China Strategy was a serious breach of the existing treaty. It was only one instance among many but it was the one which came to the notice of the Japanese public. It is of course difficult in secret diplomacy to consult partners in advance. History is strewn with such failures. But Japan has shown herself in the past to be especially sensitive to instances of secretiveness of this kind. Whenever she has entered into an alliance, she has encountered trouble. When Germany, her partner in the Anti-Comintern treaty, concluded the Nazi–Soviet Pact in August 1939, it caused the fall of the Japanese government of the day. At the earlier period of the Anglo-Japanese alliance, when Britain seemed to enter into collusion with the United States rather than consulting its ally, Japan, the latter was unforgiving. So in this case of the approach to China, Japan accepted the *fait accompli* but the United States Security Treaty has never been quite the same since.

JAPAN'S 'FREE RIDE'?

In the second half of the 1970s, Japan's security position was anomalous. It had a vast trade surplus over the United States but was militarily dependent on Washington. For their part the Americans complained that for far too long the prosperous Japanese had had 'a free ride' over defence. Perhaps this resentment came to a head with the decision of the Carter administration, when it came to power in 1977, to reduce American ground forces in South Korea. This initiative suggested to the Japanese a substantial weakening of the American–Japanese security arrangements. The fact that it was announced without consultation with them naturally caused further strains. From then on there were meetings of study teams representing Japan and the United States, and finally in 1978 they approved guidelines for Japan and US defence cooperation which would, on the one hand, guarantee close consultation in the matter of defence within the East Asian region and, on the other, make qualitative and quantitative improvements in Japan's defence capability.

Meanwhile, public opinion over Japan's security was changing. Hitherto there had been a strong pacifism among the Japanese people; but, judging from public opinion polls, there developed from about 1978 increasing support for the Japanese self-defence forces and the continuation of the security treaty with the United States. Indeed, the security issue became a topic of popular debate; and after the widespread publicity given to the annual Defence White Papers from 1976 onwards, discussions became much better informed and less polemical.

Towards the end of the Carter administration the strident American demand was that the Japanese should assume a larger share in their own defence. Just before the 1980 general elections the Japanese prime minister, then Ohira, agreed to increase the amount spent in a seemingly categorical commitment, but his successor, Mr Suzuki, was evidently less forthcoming because of domestic pressures which came from three quarters: (1) from the Ministry of Finance for budgetary reasons; (2) from the opposition in the Diet which traditionally has been opposed to heavy defence expenditure; and (3) from LDP members because they had been elected in 1980 on an electoral ticket of no increase in taxation and would be faced with a largely increased income tax bill, if the government were to go ahead with substantial defence commitments.

Understandably the Japanese resented talk of a 'free ride' which they claimed to be totally misconceived. Security, they claimed, should not be measured in financial or budgetary terms, certainly not in percentages of GNP. Japan claimed to have been loyal to the security treaty with the United States. Its government had condemned Soviet aggression in Afghanistan in December

1979 and followed the Washington line by boycotting the Olympic Games in Moscow the following summer. The two 'allies' were thus thrown together again after a period of frosty relations by increasing evidence of Soviet military–naval activity in North-East Asia. This seemed to take place after Japan had negotiated its treaty of peace and friendship with the Peoples' Republic of China in China in August 1978 (just one year before the United States). As soon as Foreign Minister Sonoda put his signature to the treaty with China, Russia concluded that Japan had in effect taken sides in the Sino-Soviet divide. Almost immediately there were signs of the Soviet Union placing new garrisons estimated at one division on the so-called Northern Territories, the island group to the north of Hokkaido which the Russians have occupied since 1945 and to which the Japanese lay claim, and increasing her naval activity in the Pacific Ocean.

When President Reagan took office, he focused attention on these Soviet activities and urged Japan to share the responsibility for defence. The new Secretary of Defense in his administration, Caspar Weinberger, reportedly told Tokyo that, unless Japanese military capability was considerably and speedily increased, opinion in Congress might make itself felt again and demand American restrictions on Japanese imports. This linkage between Japan's commercial profit and her stinginess in defence expenditure was only a repeat of an old song; but the accusation was put more pointedly than before and with a threat of counteraction. The American ambassador in Tokyo, Mike Mansfield, who had served at the embassy under President Carter and had been asked to stay on, repeated that the United States would expand its defence spending despite its own tight financial position and was relying on Japan to play 'a more positive role in specific areas'. This 'positive role in specific areas' was not spelled out. When the Suzuki Government was steering its first budget through the Diet, the Defence Agency asked for an increase of 9.7 per cent in its defence allocation for 1981. This request was reduced in cabinet to 7.61 per cent, and (according to the economic pundits) was equivalent to an increase of 3.9 per cent when adjusted for inflation. The United States put it on record that it was hoping for an increase of 15 per cent; and one of the committees within the Japanese Defence Agency said that a realistic figure would have been 20 per cent.

Prime Minister Suzuki prided himself on being a searcher for consensus in domestic affairs and harmony in Japan's overseas relations. Being preoccupied with reconciling the factions within the Liberal–Democratic party, his line in foreign affairs was often far from clear. It was not that he was unobliging to the United States, but that he did not share many of the underlying preconceptions of the incoming Reagan administration. His first mission to Washington in May 1981 led to a revelatory incident: when challenged on his return to Tokyo about the joint communiqué issued at the end of his stay on 15 May, Suzuki denied that the existence of an alliance with the United States signified an added degree of military cooperation. It was a play on words, designed to suggest that the American–Japanese security treaty did not imply a commitment on Japan to go to the aid of the United States. The embarrassment caused brought about the swift resignation of Foreign Minister Itō, who affirmed that the alliance did have clear military implications. Yet it would be wrong to conclude that Japan did not come closer to Washington under Suzuki. The Rimpac operations, naval exercises in the South Pacific region, gathered momentum under his government. The decision to enable the naval self-defence forces to operate within a 1000 sea miles perimeter from Japan's shores matured at this time. Indeed when the damaging textbook issue (which of course had no connection with the United States) arose in August 1982 under the Suzuki government, it left the impression that Japan was inclined to conceal and condone its actions earlier in the century and was in unrepentant mood. These all suggested a more militant posture. But on the most talked of issue, Suzuki would make only modest increases in the military budget. He was committed to a programme of Administrative Reform which, it was hoped, would cut down the cost of the central bureaucracy and lead to retrenchment. His other problem was Japan's accumulated budgetary debt: in order to avoid the necessity for increasing income tax, the Suzuki government decided to pare expenditure down wherever possible. It was inexpedient in such cases to concede American demands for large-scale increases in military expenditure.

THE 'RON-YASU RELATIONSHIP'

In the autumn of 1982 Mr Suzuki decided not to seek re-election as president of the Liberal–Democratic Party and thus in effect resigned from the premiership. His position was taken after a fraught period of lobbying and uncertainty by Nakasone Yasuhiro, the leader of the smallest faction in the LDP, as the result of a compromise between the major faction leaders who were deeply divided. In the presidential primary it was the supporters of former Prime Minister Tanaka whose voting power enabled Nakasone to gain a substantial majority. This brought to the prime ministership a man with a penchant for foreign affairs and defence problems, quite exceptional in postwar Japan. It also brought to the leadership one who knew the United States quite well and was arguably in some ways an American-style politician – outspoken, straightforward and concerned with his media image.

It was a matter of urgency for Nakasone to restore some of the mutual trust which had been lost in the bleak period in American–Japanese relations during the 1970s. In January 1983 he paid a special visit to the United States for discussions with President Reagan. It was reported that a new dialogue had been established and a 'special relationship' discovered. This was the 'Ron-Yasu relationship' – so called because the two statesmen were supposed to be on familiar first-name terms. Perhaps the most dramatic aspect of this visit was the press conference at which Nakasone described the Japanese islands lying off the coast of East Asia as an 'unsinkable aircraft carrier'. The intention of these remarks was to convey to American newspaper correspondents the idea that Japan was strategically sited (from an American point of view) and was a place that the United States should not neglect in her defence provisions. The phrase was 'hawkish' and one that was not welcome to the ears of the majority of Japanese for whom it was a reminder of cold war tensions. The question which this raised was whether Nakasone was presenting an attitude to the Americans which was unrepresentative of Japanese thinking and therefore misleading. Enough had, however, been said to convince the Americans that Nakasone was someone with whom they could work and who was positive in his opinions and loyal.

Most Japanese appreciated that they had in Nakasone a leader who was able to associate successfully with world leaders, as was later proved at the Williamsburg summit in May. Meanwhile the Nakasone cabinet had been addressing itself to the two major areas of American complaints: defence and trade. In the field of defence, Nakasone arranged for the defence budget to be increased by 6.5 per cent in real terms in January 1983. Perhaps the figure itself is debatable; but, considering the fact that he was introducing an austerity budget and that all around there was a call for administrative reform (which implied retrenchment), it was extraordinary that defence should have been exempted from the rigours of recessionary economic policies. Nonetheless the old American accusations about 'Japan's free ride on defence' continued to be made. The present defence build-up programme, covering the 1983–87 period, was devised to bring the defensive capability of the Self-Defence forces up to a level perceived as necessary at the beginning of the decade. The American argument has been that this improvement still ignores the substantial military build-up on the part of the Soviet Union in North-East Asia and that Japan's military spending has been slower than might have been expected. Still Secretary of Defense Caspar Weinberger recognised in a speech in June 1984:

> the increasing importance of Asia, and particularly of Japan. The increasing dangers that all of us face here, as the Soviets dramatically increase their military power in the Far East, and all of these things demand that Pacific nations be given our fullest attention in the years ahead.

If this is a mark of approval and an assurance of future support on the part of the United States, it is nonetheless impossible for Japan to ignore the criticism that it falls short in meeting the unstated obligations in the American–Japanese Security Pact. There are signs that gradually – and perhaps unconsciously – the Japanese are sharing in joint exercises with the Americans, that weapons and communications systems are being slowly but surely standardised and that Japan had agreed that exchanges of military technology may take place with the United States.

As we turn to the trade issue, we find that the world has looked with envious eyes at Japan. Engulfed by the recession years of the 1980s, the United States has suffered deficits in her trade balance with Japan and serious unemployment, while Japan has recorded surpluses. The same old complaints about Japan's trade practices have been made. While the thrust of the argument remains the same, the products in contention have differed from year to year. They have moved from synthetic textiles in the late 1960s, through merchant ships, video equipment, to cars. In 1981 the Americans passed legislation which induced the Japanese government to recommend the adoption of 'voluntary' restraint in the shipment of cars to the US for a period of three years. The numbers exported dropped substantially. A new pact was negotiated in 1984 whereby Japan extended the voluntary restraint at a slightly enhanced figure for another year, that is, until March 1985. This was clearly a desirable procedure in an election year when neither American party wanted to commit itself to the abolition of the control or its continuance. There is the suggestion that the Republicans with a stronger bent towards free trade, may differ from the Democrats who favour a greater degree of intervention because of their UAW links. On the whole, however, all parties have been inclined to leave this as an issue too sensitive to tackle for the foreseeable future.

Another attempt at alleviating the American–Japanese trade problem has been made by encouraging imports into Japan. These 'encouragement policies' covering a package of commodities ranging across the board have been greatly increased since Nakasone took office even at the expense of unpopularity in many quarters, notably agricultural opposition to the import of Californian oranges. In the face of American complaints that Japan's trade surplus was mounting again, the liberalisation process was speeded up in April 1984 and long-established tariffs were either cut or the schedule for cutting advanced. While reducing excessive exports by Japan, the government has tried to open its markets by way of import decontrol and relaxation of its remaining restrictions on imported agricultural products like beef and oranges. Nakasone has had to balance the strength of internal lobbies within the ruling party and overseas lobbies campaigning in the name of internationalism and using the threat of protectionism. But will his measures cure the trade imbalance?

Alongside these inroads into the trade sector, the United States has been intensifying her pressure for liberalisation of the banking and capital markets in Japan. This originated in President Reagan's visit to Japan in November 1983. American thinking appears to be that financial liberalisation would bring to an end, or at least reduce, the undervaluation of the *yen* of which it has

long complained and that America's large trade deficit with
Japan would be alleviated if the Japanese currency were to be
appreciated to a realistic level. The Nakasone cabinet has played
along with this pressure, however unwelcome it may have been.
The matter was referred to a Joint Ad Hoc Committee (the *yen*-
dollar Committee) which seemed to reach a tolerable agreement
in Washington in April 1984 and cemented this at a final session
in Rome in the following month. The Japanese agreed to a
lengthy series of measures which cannot fail to have far-reaching
repercussions for Japan's financial structure and may force the
yen to face greater responsibilities as a world currency. Inevitably
Japanese banks and security companies will have to face
increased competition. From the issues we have raised in the
last five paragraphs, it might appear that Nakasone has bowed
before American pressure on several issues of political
significance. In return, Japan and Nakasone can claim to have
gained prestige. At the Williamsburg summit in May 1983,
Japan was accorded a special place as one of the leading
industrial democracies and had established an unquestioned
right to sit at the top table and take part in coordinating
high policy for world economic recovery. At the same time,
Williamsburg seems to have confirmed Nakasone as the first
Japanese prime minister who was able to establish a rapport
with world leaders. In particular he emerged as the main
supporter of American proposals at the conference. The 'Ron-
Yasu relationship' was developed. But it has to be remembered
that the Japanese in the 1970s learnt to adopt a *jishū gaikō* – an
autonomous diplomacy. This does not allow Japan to fall too
much under the American shadow. Instead the Japanese want
to keep their distance and sustain a posture of diplomatic
independence which is commensurate with their economic status
in the world.

Towards the end of 1983 Nakasone was hit by domestic crises
of various kinds, most importantly from the court verdict against
his political sponsor, Tanaka. For political reasons it was
necessary for him to go to the country. But in the general election
of 18 December Nakasone's party experienced a reverse in the
lower house of the Diet. He managed to repair this by a political
alliance with the breakaway New Liberal Club which gave him
a voting strength almost equal to that of the combined opposition
parties (who were in any case divided). This difficult crisis was

unquestionably damaging for Nakasone personally and for his prospects as party president. But it caused him to modify some of his policies and this has made him more popular. The other point that needs to be made is that, while the Tanaka case and the state of the LDP contributed to this electoral upset, it was not Nakasone's policy of commitment to the American alliance that was in question nor his role as a world statesman. It was domestic issues that called the tune and foreign successes could not be used to counterbalance the basic unpopularity of the ministry's internal policies. In 1984 Nakasone's international image as a world statesman had risen through his mission to China in March and his appearance at the London summit in June. Even then he had to beat a swift retreat to Japan to attend to a domestic crisis. But he was successful in the election for the party presidency in November despite the faction in-fighting that erupted.

CONCLUSION

If we examine Japan's perception of America during the 1980s we can detect two changes which have taken place in the relationship. In the first place, there has been a marked change in Japan's perception of her role in the world. As Prime Minister Nakasone said in a speech delivered in London in 1984:

as the world underwent major structural changes, it became clear that Japan could not simply keep on responding passively to changing circumstances. Japan's position demanded that we work actively for world peace and prosperity. Despite Japan's best efforts, when I assumed the office of Prime Minister in 1982, the situation was serious. A vast gap still existed between Japanese reality and what the rest of the world expected of Japan. One of the first things I did in office was to address the people on Japan's need to move toward an 'international nation' – a nation that bears responsibilities in keeping with its international position.

It may be that not every Japanese sees his country's destiny this way. It may be too that the Japanese at the Williamsburg and London summits have not been as outspoken as this policy statement would suggest. But it is something that the Japanese prime minister should preach the doctrine of Japan's global political role in line with her commercial position in the world and should emphasise it despite the fact that Japan cannot be on the top rung of military powers.

In the second place, there has been a subtle change in the business of Japanese diplomacy. Whereas ten years ago the intercourse of the Japanese Foreign Ministry was economic and commercial in the main, issues more appropriate for the economic commentator, Japan is now consulted and expresses views on political issues. It is not just that world leaders join in a procession to visit Tokyo and that Japanese ministers find it necessary to pay regular visits to foreign capitals. There is in addition the fact that Japan sees herself as having a role for Asia as the only Asian country to have an undisputed right to sit at the top table. The regular meetings between Japanese and American cabinet ministers which seemed to become less frequent in the 1970s have been restored. There may, of course, be a fallacy in the notion that the mere act of meeting regularly will lead to the solution of all problems. Many of the problems between them, especially in the trade field, are fairly intractable ones. But there is a new range of issues on which Japan has a right to be heard – East–West tensions, the North–South problem, cooperation between the Pacific Basin countries, to name but a few – and there is a considerable need for political dialogue between the United States and Japan.

There are two basic ingredients in American–Japanese relations. There is the security treaty between the two; and there have been shrill complaints in the past that Japan has not assisted Washington in countering its relative military decline. It would appear that the Reagan administration now has greater confidence on that head; but there are still voices critical of Japan's idea of comprehensive security. The other is the economic relationship; and here too the United States has suffered a relative decline. In the days of recession, as American unemployment figures rose sharply, the population at large were tempted to attribute much of the blame to the Japanese surpluses in bilateral trade. Administrations may accept that trade disputes are disputes between private interests which should not be allowed to disturb the relations between two nation states. But they do make news; and they do appeal to public opinion and emotion in democratic societies. For this reason there has been over the past decade unrelenting American pressure against the allegedly protectionist trade practices of the Japanese domestic market. Many of these practices have with difficulty been eliminated or modified. It is too much to hope that these trade disputes will disappear in the future. But the steps that have been taken will make it easier in future to monitor the disputes and resolve them. In this way, the United States – and Europe which operates in her shadow in these matters – may find the relationship more satisfying. The American–Japanese alliance which has known its ups and downs over its thirty-year history might then come back on course.

4   The Soviet Union in East Asia

GERALD SEGAL

The Soviet Union is the most powerful state in East Asia, as it is in Europe. Yet, while the Soviet Union is European in outlook, it is not a natural East Asian state. Although Russian history is closely related to European history, the extension of Russian power to the Pacific is relatively recent. Therefore, consideration of Soviet policy in East Asia must begin with the essential Soviet predicament – it is *the* power in East Asia, but it is not an East Asian power.

This and other predicaments of Soviet power in East Asia assume added urgency if the Soviet Union is to take an active part in the coming 'Pacific century'. On the one hand, as an East Asian power, the Soviet Union could be expected to begin with basic advantages over its Superpower rival. However, unlike the United States, Moscow has not developed a tight web of economic and political links with local states. This failure is both a result of errors in Soviet policy, and a reflection of Moscow's fundamental dilemmas.

POLITICS AND IDEOLOGY

In political and ideological terms, East Asia is both less important and more complex than Europe for Soviet policy-makers. In Europe, the Soviet Union is flanked by communist states of mixed reliability who provide both political support and ideological justification for Soviet Superpower claims. In East Asia, Moscow has only Mongolian loyalty and unstable support from North Korea, Vietnam, Laos and Kampuchea. The 'enemy'

44

in Europe is the easily identifiable advanced and fairly stable capitalist states of Western Europe, supported by close and tangible cooperation with the United States. In East Asia the picture is far more unstable and defies simple ideological categories. An independent but weak and often erratic China is Moscow's major concern. Just offshore is the Japanese economic giant but of limited political consequence. Further offshore, but never far from Soviet concerns is United States power and influence. Lastly there are scattered states of varying political importance, including South Korea, Taiwan, and South-East Asian regimes, united in fearing that Soviet influence might choke their economic future.

Unlike the United States which built political bridges to many East Asian states, the Soviet Union has remained an outsider. The reasons for this weakness are many. They include the Soviets' lingering imperial frame of mind towards their relatively new East Asian territories, and an inflexible ideological framework that does not appreciate the special problems of development in Third World and culturally different states. Above all, the Soviet Union has not made East Asia a priority, focusing instead on the European and Superpower balance.

Yet for all these problems, the view from Moscow also reveals some positive perspectives. The recent extension of Soviet power to East Asia means that there is little of the deep-rooted hostility that states like Poland hold for Russian policy. Similarly, Moscow's barely veiled sense of inferiority about Europe's culture and technology does not seem to apply in East Asia. To the extent that general Soviet foreign policy is derived from insecurity, Moscow might therefore be expected to exhibit more confidence about East Asia. In addition, the Soviet Union, unlike the United States, does have at least part of its population of Asian stock which might serve to build political bridges to states of the area. The Soviet argument that the United States does not belong in Europe has always been undermined by close ethnic, cultural and ideological links between America and Europe. In East Asia, such accusations might well be expected to carry greater weight. Yet despite these positive aspects, it is striking how little progress Moscow has made in becoming accepted as a natural East Asian state.

MILITARY ISSUES

The Soviet Union also has serious dilemmas regarding East Asian military affairs. Despite the advantage of having considerable forces in East Asia, the Soviet Union has little confidence that it has anything but a minimum defence force. The reasons for this sense of weakness are both practical, and theoretical.

In practical terms, the Soviet Union has no defensive glacis like the Warsaw Pact. With the exception of Mongolia, Soviet troops directly face superior numbers of Chinese troops on land, and the technologically advanced naval forces of the United States and Japan at sea. The Soviet frontier in East Asia is its longest and is reinforced by vulnerable logistic lines. Soviet East Asia is also relatively under-populated, but faces China which has no shortage of manpower.

It is true that in recent years the Soviet Union has developed important military base facilities in South-East Asia, but they depend on unreliable allies. Soviet naval installations in Vietnam are mostly temporary, for no doubt Soviet planners remember the lessons of their unstable relationship with China and their expulsion from Egypt and Somalia in the 1970s. It is also true that Soviet forces in East Asia have been improved and expanded, but few analysts would suggest that they have superiority over their likely regional opponents. The Soviet Union continues to have special problems in reinforcing its Pacific fleet, not to mention vulnerability to being bottled up in port because of naval choke points.

To make matters worse from the Soviet military planners' perspective, there are also more deeply ingrained reasons from Soviet defence culture that would encourage a pessimistic view. The Soviet tendency to rely on numbers rather than technology for defence encourages a perception of weakness against a more populous China. What is more, the Soviet concept of alliance is not one that accepts others as equals, and therefore tends to view anything that is not obedience as hostility. While Mongolian passivity is by and large pleasing to Soviet planners, even in that case there are grounds to doubt that Mongolia will continue to be perfectly passive. Such allies as the more independent North Koreans or Vietnamese hardly inspire Soviet confidence.

The Soviet invasion of Afghanistan, while strictly speaking outside the realm of this analysis, has also had an impact on

Soviet military plans in East Asia. It encouraged greater hostility from China and reinforced the view in South-East Asia that the Soviet Union was a predatory power. Moscow thereby lost some of the tacit gains it had made after the February 1979 Chinese attack on Vietnam. The Soviet defence culture of encirclement by hostile states may well have encouraged the Soviet Union to invade Afghanistan, but it also resulted in a self-fulfilling prophecy of encirclement.

ECONOMIC ISSUES

The Soviet Union does share the notion of a Pacific century in that it sees an important future for development of Soviet East Asia. The need for new resources, for new population to balance the decline in the birth rate and the need for an *entrée* into the future development of the international Pacific economic region, all encourage Soviet planners to pay new attention to its East Asian territories.

Not so long ago, Moscow expected some foreign, and especially Japanese, cooperation in expanding East Asian Siberia and tapping its mineral resources. However, the dreams of a Siberian bonanza have not been fulfilled. The reasons are many, but in the forefront must be the hard facts of economic cost-effectiveness. While there are undoubtedly important resources in Soviet East Asia, they are simply too expensive to be exploited given contemporary market prices. In addition, political considerations make the Japanese and the Americans less likely to take the economic risk.

Therefore the Soviet Union's economic relations with East Asia remain relatively frozen. On the one hand the Soviet Union has trading relationships with Mongolia, Korea and its allies in South-East Asia akin to that between developed and developing nations. On the other hand, in relations with Japan the roles are reversed and the Soviet Union is the 'developing' state.

The great China market is only now beginning to show signs of development, but the Soviet Union has not yet formulated a strategy for expansion of Sino-Soviet trade. In many senses both are more natural competitors rather than cooperators in trade, sharing natural resources and yet little high technology to exploit the wealth. The place that China once held in Soviet trade as the paramount developing nation, has since been supplanted by newer Third World allies. Any return to large scale Sino-Soviet trade will inevitably require a Soviet decision to harm the interests of some allies.

Perhaps the most important dilemma for Soviet policy is more general – whether to engage in domestic economic reform. To fail to do so will probably mean more muddling through, but less prospect of developing East Asian Siberia or trade relations with local states. Such a soft option may, however, only remain soft in the short term. In the medium term, the Soviet Union will run up against the hard economic facts that smaller growth will lead to economic shortages and political instability. While there may have been some prospect of a Soviet Pacific century behind Andropov's reforms, Chernenko's stifling of reform did set the optimists back. The new Gorbachev leadership will have to confront the economic dilemmas, just as they will have to face the predicaments in military and political terms. Unfortunately for the Soviet Union, there does not seem to be any simple solutions. To a certain extent the balance of preferences depends on which bilateral relations Moscow considers.

SINO-SOVIET RELATIONS

In most respects, Sino-Soviet relations are the key to Soviet strategy in East Asia. By virtue of its size, distinct (if changing) ideology and economic potential, China remains the most important East Asian actor. But this 'fact' of East Asian international politics is not nearly as difficult for Soviet policy as the fact that China's policy has rarely been static. Indeed, the major problems in Sino-Soviet relations can be traced to changes in Chinese policy.

Soviet policy towards China has remained remarkably consistent. That is not to suggest that there are no differences of opinion in the Kremlin about China, or that Soviet policy has never changed, and above all that Moscow is not to blame for any deterioration in relations. But in most cases, fluctuations of policy came first from a China in search of its proper domestic and international role.

Sino-Soviet relations since the death of Mao Zedong have been no exception to this pattern. The gradual amelioration of relations, especially since 1980, have their deepest roots in Chinese domestic politics. Beijing's objective of the Four Modernisations required greater pragmatism at home, and a more peaceful international environment. Therefore the previous Chinese dogmatism about the Soviet threat to China was reassessed. In its place came a new realism that minimised the urgency and potency of the Soviet challenge, and staked out greater independence for China between the Superpowers. The basic dimensions of the original Sino-Soviet split moved slowly, but emphatically from conflict towards cooperation.

First, China's new experiments with domestic reform meant a lessening of ideological hostility towards Soviet communism. Gone were the days of Chinese epithets of 'goulash communism' or 'Soviet revisionism'. China's experiments with East European innovations of the Soviet model and new incentives for economic production led to the ending of all major recriminations with Moscow and its allies on domestic policies.

China even made overtures for the re-establishment of some party-to-party relations with East European regimes, but that process was blocked by a Soviet Union reluctant to be seen to sell out the interests of fellow communist allies such as Vietnam and Afghanistan. In fact, by 1984 and the death of Andropov, it became clear that further improvement in this domestic and party dimension of Sino-Soviet relations was being blocked by the Soviet Union rather than China. For the first time in decades, Moscow rather than Beijing was holding back Sino-Soviet *détente*.

Second, the military confrontation has eased, with no reported border clashes for four years. What is more remarkable about this military *détente*, is that it comes while both sides have increased and improved their military capability. The explanation for the seemingly contradictory trends is to be found in the evolving defence cultures of both states. China's assessment of the Soviet threat is based on more than just hardware. China's confidence about its ability to deter the Soviet threat by raising the cost of an attack to the invader is founded on more intangible elements of military modernisation. Greater professionalism, and the improvement in military doctrine has even made possible a reduction in the size of the Chinese army. Beijing's defence culture is also based on a more general assessment of the Soviet threat, and in the 1980s China came to recognise that Soviet power was more limited and the Soviet economy less healthy than previously believed.

Soviet defence culture has changed more ambiguously. On the one hand, Moscow is encouraged by the general diminution of China's anti-Soviet rhetoric and its return to a more understandable form of communist politics. The Chinese decision to pursue independent military modernisation rather than rely on arms purchases from abroad has also reassured those Soviet ideologues and military analysts fearful of a grand anti-Soviet coalition. But less positively, the elements of Soviet defence culture that see no sufficiency in military equipment encourage further deployments when none is really required.

For the time being, Sino-Soviet defence culture has largely served to encourage a modicum of *détente*, but it may soon serve to block any further relaxation of tension. Without some concrete evidence of reduction in troops, equipment and tension, neither side will feel confident enough to move further forward. The time has come for both sides to demonstrate that their mutually professed desires for military *détente* is more than mere rhetoric.

Third, there has been a demonstrable improvement in economic relations. Trade levels have risen from their pathetic levels of the 1970s and the signs are strong that both sides are prepared to move forward in this dimension even if there is deadlock on other issues. Of course both sides have yet to resolve important economic questions, for example on the extent to which they wish to refurbish old equipment provided by the Soviet Union and their allies in the 1950s.

Fourth, both sides have adopted a more even-handed attitude towards each other's relations with the United States. China's abandonment of its extreme anti-Sovietism of the 1970s and Moscow's greater tolerance for a mixture of cooperation and conflict in Sino-American relations, has meant that there is more room for manoeuvre in the great power triangle. To be sure, the Soviet Union remains acutely concerned about signs of a Sino-American coalition, but Chinese statements and actions in the past few years have indicated that China's foreign policy of independence is more than words.

Fifth, there has been some easing of relations regarding conflict in the Third World. In non-Asian areas, Moscow and Beijing see far more eye-to-eye on the nature of events than they have for decades. While Moscow emphasises the United States' culpability for conflict, China is at least willing to acknowledge that the United States is often the *main* problem, while noting that both Superpowers carry some responsibility.

In Asia, the conflicts in South-East Asia and Afghanistan continue to hamper Sino-Soviet *détente*. China insists on Soviet troop withdrawals from Afghanistan and a Vietnamese withdrawal from Kampuchea (and/or a withdrawal of Soviet support for Vietnam) as preconditions to further Sino-Soviet *détente*. China links its third precondition, the diminution of the threat along the frontier, to the other two and insists it cannot be resolved *before* some progress is seen on Vietnam and Afghanistan.

The limits to Sino-Soviet *détente* are therefore numerous and complex. China's notion of preconditions seems both unreasonable and unfair, for its suggests far more Soviet control over events than is really the case. It also prevents a modicum of *détente*, say on the frontier, where a bilateral agreement may be possible. Moscow bears the burden of blame to a lesser extent in that since the death of Andropov it has held back the normalisation of relations by postponing the Arkhipov visit from May until December 1984, and for a time stepped up the level of polemical exchanges about Chinese foreign policy. No doubt instability in the Soviet leadership was an important part of the explanation for this policy.

Yet in a longer perspective, there are strong reasons for at least a creeping normalisation of Sino-Soviet relations. Both sides require and seem to desire some reduction in their military burdens. Both wish to retain leverage against the United States and therefore require some tangible signs of Sino-Soviet *détente*. Both also want a more peaceful international environment and cannot be pleased that relatively peripheral issues, like Afghanistan and Vietnam, are blocking the way.

Thus the logic of a *détente* that leaves some issues unresolved – competitive coexistence – seems compelling. However, the issues are complex enough, the leaderships are insecure enough and both powers are proud and paranoid enough to allow their great power aspirations to stymie the logic of Sino-Soviet *détente*. Such a missed opportunity serves neither the interests of Beijing nor Moscow.

SOVIET–AMERICAN RELATIONS

Soviet–American relations are of course Moscow's dominant foreign policy concern. But in the East Asian context, the Soviet Union has reason to be relatively more sanguine about Superpower confrontation. To be sure, both powers face each other in the theatre with powerful nuclear and conventional arms and neither can afford to ignore each other's presence. But in comparison to the European theatre where the troops are toe-to-toe along the world's most heavily armed frontier, East Asia is a lesser priority.

The reasons for this relative Soviet sanguinity are complex. Above all, United States power is largely offshore, there are no direct land confrontations of Superpower troops, and the Soviet Union offers few 'high value' targets in East Asia. This is not to suggest that the Soviet Union is unconcerned about its own territorial integrity in East Asia, American naval power in the Pacific or its bases in Japan, Korea and the Philippines. But the trend in the last decade has largely been for the removal of United States troops from Asian territory. Certainly the dangers posed by the Korean and Vietnamese wars have largely passed. Of course, the Reagan administration has clouded this Soviet confidence by building up American naval forces in the Pacific, and halting the retreat from South Korea.

Equally, Soviet forces have been modernised while the Americans agonised over their Pacific posture. While Moscow has nothing near superiority in military power in the theatre, it certainly has not fallen further behind. However, this rough parity in a perplexing military equation leaves little room for arms control. Unlike the European theatre where various types of arms control are both possible and necessary, in East Asia both Superpowers have settled for moderate modernisation of relatively defensive deployments. The military state of affairs might even serve as a useful example of managing competitive coexistence with China, or with the Europeans in the West.

Unfortunately, and unlike the European situation, the lines dividing Soviet and American interests in East Asia are fuzzy. Cold war containment lines have always been less clear in Asia, primarily because such world views were not applicable to the complex local conditions. The process of adapting to instability has been protracted and bloody. Both powers were singed by the Korean and Vietnamese wars, with the Americans being burned far more badly. The shifts in China's position between the Superpowers also undermined the notion of stable cold war lines. Most importantly, powerful nationalisms of South-East Asian states frustrated great power attempts at manipulation.

The complex local conditions are likely to continue to be a cause of instability for Superpowers who continue to doubt that their power is limited. Paranoid military planners will continue to argue that more forces are needed in the area. But a review of the Soviet position in the East Asian Superpower balance reveals a consolidation of Moscow's position and if anything a retreat of United States power. The Soviet Union can be mostly satisfied with the parity it has achieved.

SOVIET–JAPANESE RELATIONS

The Soviet Union's conduct of Soviet–Japanese relations has been remarkably consistent, but consistently shortsighted. With the exception of a brief spell during the 1970s, Moscow has regularly slammed doors and cut off options that might have led to an important Soviet–Japanese *détente*. It is difficult to fathom why the errors were made.

Certainly some of the elements of Soviet defence culture, insecurity and lack of confidence, that afflict Sino–Soviet relations, do not apply in the Japanese case. Russian troops have posed an overwhelming threat to Japan since they trounced the Imperial army in Manchuria in 1945. Japan's defence forces remain puny, even including direct American support. (Compare Japan with that other American offshore ally, the United Kingdom.)

The positive attractions of dealing with a Japanese economic power-house must be enormous for the Soviet Union. Japanese technology is the equal of that from Western Europe. Yet trade with Japan must appear more positive in Moscow because it would be less likely to help build up an effective political opponent. Japan's political influence in East Asia remains constrained by the memories of Japanese imperialism in the 1930–40s and its relative lack of military clout. It seems only logical for the Soviet Union to try to entice Japan into a closer relationship and undermine the United States' 'unsinkable aircraft carrier' in East Asia.

However, there are strong limits to Soviet–Japanese *détente*. In the political realm there is the enduring Soviet suspicion that Japan is merely a puppet of American power. However, Soviet fears seem exaggerated. One merely need reflect on Japanese–American economic disputes to see that Japan has in many senses come of political age. The trend towards full Japanese independence gathers momentum yearly. Tokyo's increasing political role in East Asia is in part because it is a successful Asian state rather than a spearhead of American influence.

In military terms, the Japanese–American alliance remains firm. But to a large extent it is based on a shared perception of the Soviet threat, something merely reinforced by Soviet intransigence. Moscow's muddled policies on the disputed northern islands offers Japanese friends of the Soviet Union little encouragement. In Europe, Soviet–German relations improved and American–German relations deteriorated, when Moscow helped give Bonn some of the political independence and satisfaction on inter-German issues that had been denied by the previous hostile atmosphere. Perhaps Moscow is awaiting similar approaches from the Japanese. But conversely, Moscow could help cut Japan's American anchor by some concessions on the disputed islands.

In the economic realm, the limits on trade are largely to be found in the objective difficulty in exploiting resources in Soviet East Asia. In addition, Japan would have to treat the Soviet Union as a developing nation for much of its trade. Not only would this pose problems from the Soviet perspective, but it would be unacceptable to Japan to be too heavily dependent on the Soviet Union for strategic resources.

On balance, the state of Soviet–Japanese and Soviet–Chinese relations share important resemblances. In both cases, the Soviet Union must perceive a powerful logic for *détente*. That Moscow refuses to explore the logic of *détente* says a great deal about deeply ingrained Soviet insecurity and its sense of not belonging to East Asia. In the end, to persist in both beliefs will become a self-fulfilling prophecy.

SOVIET–KOREAN RELATIONS

Soviet–Korean relations are a mirror of Soviet East Asian

relations. Sino-Soviet competition for influence in North Korea is similar to Moscow's main concern in the region. After decades of waxing and waning of influence, both communist powers have settled for limited influence in Pyongyang. American support for South Korea and the Soviet support for North Korea has led both Superpowers into crisis, but both have also learned to minimise the dangers of alliances with unstable irredentist allies.

Soviet–Korean relations, like many general Soviet attitudes towards the area, remain marginal for Moscow. But relations with Korea cannot be abandoned. In Sino-Soviet terms, both communist powers continue to curry favour with Pyongyang in the hope that the Kim Il Sung succession may favour their position. Neither communist power wishes to become embroiled in a war to unite Korea, but neither can risk antagonising North Korea by abandoning support for the ideal of unification.

Moscow's main military concern about Korea centres on the risks of war with the United States. The Soviet Union has grown accustomed to controlling North Korean provocations, and assuming a restrained position when the United States responded. In 1983 the roles were somewhat reversed when Moscow shot down a KAL 747 and yet there was no significant American reaction. Of course the incident raised a howl of protests, but these merely mirrored the general deterioration of East–West relations. It also mirrored the essential robustness of deterrence and stability in the military confrontation.

The Soviet Union's economic attitude to Korea is that it is little more than a drain that has to be filled for political reasons. It is also a symbol of the essential failure of the Soviet Union to develop any serious economic relations with East Asia. Compared with the massive American role in the area, the Soviet Union is not a serious economic actor.

SOVIET–SOUTH-EAST ASIAN RELATIONS

South-East Asia is the most remote portion of the theatre for the Soviet Union. Yet Moscow has been involved in local events for decades, albeit not as directly as the United States. Soviet involvement, pre-eminently in the Vietnam war, resulted from the entry of the United States, including over 500,000 soldiers. It was also fed by a Soviet concern with Chinese influence in the area, and as an extension of the Sino-Soviet split. With the retreat of the United States in the 1970s, the Soviet concern with China became paramount.

South-East Asia, and an alliance with Vietnam, offered Moscow certain important benefits. First, it provided worry for Chinese defence planners of the possibility of Soviet encirclement. Second, Moscow obtained military bases and helped counter long-standing American deployments in the area and newer deployments in the Indian Ocean. Although Soviet bases are still not permanent, they are important in helping break out of the limits imposed by the choke points of the Soviet Pacific fleet. Third, Soviet influence in Vietnam means that as Vietnamese control expanded in South-East Asia, to a certain extent Soviet influence went with it.

Needless to say, the Soviet perception is also clouded by important problems. First, the spread of the Sino-Soviet conflict to South-East Asia that so pleased Moscow in time of Sino-Soviet hostility, now serves as a major obstacle to Sino-Soviet *détente* in the less antagonistic mood of the 1980s. Second, the price paid for Soviet bases is an enormous economic bill for supporting Vietnam and its Kampuchean occupation. In addition, Vietnam's involvement in Comecon has caused unrest in the organisation and required even more Soviet aid. The far from flush Soviet economy could do without these drains. Lastly, just as the spread of Vietnam's influence is the spread of Soviet influence, so the spread of antagonism towards Vietnam in South-East Asia also harms Soviet attempts to build political bridges to the non-communist states of the area.

The predicaments are plain. It is notable that they exist almost without any reference to the Superpower balance, and are related to Sino-Soviet and regional complexities. Yet these are more than sufficient to befuddle Soviet calculations. Before the death of Andropov, and in line with the optimistic trends of Sino-Soviet relations, there were some signs that Moscow was prepared to 'bite the bullet' and cut back some support for Vietnam in the hope of improving Sino-Soviet relations. However, those faint hopes virtually faded from sight with the shortsighted and often xenophobic reactions of the unstable Chernenko administration and have not revived under Gorbachev.

In the short term, there can therefore be little confidence that Moscow will risk losing its Vietnamese bases by pursuing a more adventurous *détente* with China. While the door to this adventurous policy may well remain open for some time, it is more likely that change will come from other avenues. For example, if Vietnam slowly consolidates its hold on Kampuchea and its economy gradually stabilises, Hanoi may well seek greater independence from Moscow in the hope of obtaining more diverse foreign aid. On the other hand, if China sees its policy of bleeding Vietnam has failed, it may well abandon the Vietnam precondition for Sino-Soviet *détente*.

These eventualities may be remote, but at least some offer hope to the Kremlin that others will simplify their South-East Asian predicaments. However, the risk of such passivity is of course that Moscow will once again fall victim to an independent-minded Vietnamese government and find itself with neither bases nor *détente* with China. If that is the outcome, Soviet leaders will only have themselves to blame.

TOWARDS A SOVIET PACIFIC CENTURY?

While the United States can look forward to a possible 'Pacific century', the Soviet Union looks like having more to fear. Although East Asia appears less dangerous to the Soviet Union than Europe, it also appears more complex and less important. Moscow might respond to this problem by assuming a more innovative foreign policy, including overtures to China and Japan. Although such policy carries the risk of de-stabilisation, Moscow runs the greater risk of having policy problems shaped by others if it insists on merely muddling through.

For example, failure to pursue *détente* with China may encourage a second attempt at a Chinese–American–Japanese alliance. Wars in Korea or Vietnam may still take place, and in a sullen xenophobic mood, the Soviet Union may find itself with unwanted commitments and dangers. The choice between positive policies and passivity is of course similar to the question faced by the Soviet leadership in domestic politics. The escape from Moscow's muddle may well have to await clarification of direction in internal politics.

Some Soviet planners might suggest that a build-up of Soviet military power is the only answer. However, as the Soviet Union has found elsewhere in the Third World, this will also not resolve the problems. Indeed, it may well drive the East Asians further away. In any case, the Soviet Union probably cannot afford a sharp increase in military deployments, especially for an area that has almost limitless scope for paranoid military planners.

In the end, if the Soviet Union is to have any hope of taking part in, and advantage of the Pacific century, it will have to reform both its domestic and foreign policy. Soviet claims to international prominence that accompany Superpower status have to be earned, not merely asserted or demanded at bayonet point.

Part II
Regional Powers and Regional Conflicts

5 China: An International Power?

BRIAN BEEDHAM

'China; is it an international power?' My answer to that is 'Not really, not for a long time'. Since that is, on the whole, a minority position, I have justification for what will follow. But before I expand my argument I should explain that I have been to China only twice in my life, though for reasonably long periods. I follow the affairs of China with interest and in many ways with affection and admiration. I do not speak or read Chinese and I am not one of that breed known as Sinologists, men and women capable of spending a day up to their ears in the *People's Daily* and the *Reference News*.

Even if I were a China expert, I would still have to make another cautionary disclaimer, because of the limitations of what it is possible to know about China. These limitations are those of Chinese statistics, which have to be treated with even more of a raised eyebrow than those of most other communist countries. They are also limitations of politics, because the Chinese experience of the past 30 years has been an attempt to apply the ideas of a German intellectual – Marx – to an eastern society which has the longest continuous tradition of a single language and a single political entity of any place in the world, and that is bound to produce confusions which may often baffle the outsider. Moreover, even the dedicated and experienced Sinologist when going to China faces considerable limitations on freedom of movement. Not long ago I sat down with a colleague and worked out that for the enormous majority of foreigners travelling to China, it was possible, at the time, to visit only about 15 cities and perhaps, we calculated, up to about 100 communes in the countryside – a fraction of one per cent of their total number.

That said, my proposition is that China is not a Superpower. It is not even a medium power in most people's definition of that term. In economic terms, which are usually at the root of things, the Chinese gross national product is roughly the size of Britain's – but it has to support a population not of 50 million but of 1000 million.

China is a very special place, unlike anywhere else, in a category of its own. It has the advantages of sheer size and numbers, but numbers can be a burden as well as an advantage. It possesses nuclear weapons, but like other possessors of such weapons it finds their actual utility limited. China has great weaknesses in its economy; great weaknesses in its military forces; a special weakness of geography, in that it is contiguous to the Soviet Union, the major military power in the world today; and the weakness of an unstable political system.

My thesis is that China is best and most simply described as a giant without legs. I will argue the leglessness of China under the heading of three propositions: first, that it has an unsolved political crisis; second, that it has an unsolved economic crisis; and, third, that it has recently developed a new crisis of ideology, or political identity.

THE POLITICAL PROBLEM

First, then, the unsolved political crisis, or the sad story of what went wrong in the first place; and then what went wrong with the attempt to put right what had gone wrong; and then what went wrong with the attempt to put that right; and the mess left behind by this triple failure.

What went wrong in the first instance, of course, was the simple fact of a one-party system that Lenin created in 1917. It is sometimes forgotten that the one-party system was not an invention of Marx. It was an invention of Lenin, against the opposition of people like Rosa Luxembourg, and having been imposed by Lenin on the Soviet Union after 1917 it was dutifully adopted by every country which took up the Marxist philosophy afterwards. That single party structure, by concentrating all power over virtually every aspect of the country's life in the hands of a single party, inevitably led to a concentration of this power in the hands of a small group of generally rather elderly people at the top of that party. It also created at the level below the top – in the bureaucracy, the people who actually do the day-to-day administration of the country – a sycophancy, a nervousness, a dullness, a tendency to obey orders above everything else, which produces a really appalling degree of inefficiency.

The great thing that can be said for Chairman Mao is that he recognised this weakness of the one-party system and decided to do something about it. That is enormously to his credit. But instead of meeting the problem head-on, and accepting that the essence of the problem was the one-party system itself, he attempted to solve the problem by cleansing the one party from within. He maintained the system but tried to renovate it by imitating Trotsky's idea of permanent revolution. He instituted in 1966, with the Cultural Revolution, the concept that the one-party system could clear out its tubes about once a generation by a huge upheaval from below, which would revive it and make it efficient again.

The result was, pretty predictably, chaos. The Red Guards, the body of Chinese youth which Chairman Mao called out in the Cultural Revolution to cleanse the party from within, divided, sub-divided, and re-sub-divided, each group trying to out-vie the others in revolutionary zeal. The outcome was a series of local civil wars, of which we are only just beginning to hear the details, and the casualty list of which may well amount to as many as half a million people. Universities were closed for three or four years. The school system was half-destroyed by the belief that revolutionary zeal mattered more than being expert or educated. Production in industry plummeted for the same reason. China fell into a shambles, lasting about ten years, which would have gone on even longer if Mrs Mao's attempt to create a second cultural revolution in the mid-1970s had been allowed to take place.

In fact, it was nipped in the bud by that minority of the Chinese leadership which realised that this was nonsense and had to be stopped. This group, centred around Deng Xiaoping, includes a number of other elderly and courageous men who realised that Mao's attempt to solve the problem that Lenin bequeathed was itself a disaster. In order to arrest the phenomenon, they seized Mrs Mao and her allies; they re-created order; they gave back priority to expertise and to standards; they restored incentives to industry and to the countryside. Perhaps more important than anything else, they created a new slogan which is implicity a challenge to the idea of Leninism: 'Experience is the only test of truth.' It is a slogan which can be heard almost everywhere in China. It means, in effect, applying to everything the question, 'Does it work?'. It is a slogan which sums up the whole philosophy of pragmatism, and pragmatism and Marxism do not live easily side by side.

The minority which tried to repair the damage done by Mao's cultural revolution nevertheless found on their hands an unresolved crisis, for two reasons.

First, at the top level, among the leadership, there were too few people wholly and dedicatedly committed to the idea of this attempt to put things right. Deng and his group, in order to institute their policies, had to make an alliance and therefore a compromise with a second group of people in the post-Mao leadership. They were able to dispense with what might be called the romantic extreme left, but they had to make a compromise with the people in the middle – the men who had thought that perhaps there was something to be said for what Mao had been trying to do, or, even more important, who had gained in position and influence during the Mao period. Therefore, at the very top, from the beginning of this counter attack by Deng and company, there was a flaw at the core – the alliance with the compromisers.

Second, below this top-level problem, there was a second and even greater problem at what might be called the non-commissioned officer level of the Chinese system – the level of the party and government officials who actually run the country from day to day.

I well remember a number of experiences in my trips to China which vividly illustrate the psychological chaos left behind by the Cultural Revolution. There is, first of all, the bitterness of the enormous numbers of people who suffered, often physically, at the hands of the Cultural Revolution. When we were in Sichuan our party of five English journalists was provided, with a subtlety that still puzzles me, with a Chinese translator who spoke only German. Fortunately, my wife, who is Swiss, was able to talk to him, though nobody else could. She was given his story. In 1966, at the beginning of the Cultural Revolution, he had just finished his training in German to be a translator, and had just got married. Within six months of the beginning of the

Cultural Revolution he and his wife had both been arrested, not for anything that they had done but because they both came from middle-class backgrounds and were genetically suspect. He was sent to work in a factory, sweeping the factory floor. His wife was sent to a punishment camp 500 miles away. Ten years later the Cultural Revolution finally came to an end, and they were both still in their factories. Even after the end of the Cultural Revolution, it took another three years before their repeated letters and appeals received any attention and they were at last free to come back to their home city, meet each other again and attempt to resume, after 13 years, a normal life and a normal marriage.

There are millions of people of about that age in China who had something like that experience and are now filled with a profound bitterness about it. Fox Butterfield, the *New York Times* correspondent, tells a story of meeting a young girl in a Chinese park, who said her father was a high party official. But she and her generation would not dream of marrying a party man because, she said, 'We would have to ask ourselves, whom did he sell in order to get his party place?' That kind of disillusionment and bitterness is one of the costs of the Cultural Revolution.

The second kind is the opposite. The Cultural Revolution was organised by Mao, and Mao's infantry were the Red Guards, young people aged between 17 and 25, who, for a number of years, had the most exhilarating experiences of their lives or any possible life they could now imagine. For a time they were the favoured of Chairman Mao, wandering over the face of China as the privileged makers of revolution. The new men have now brought this to an end. The second political problem of contemporary China is this residue of possibly millions of young people who think that Mao was right, that Mao gave them a great deal of fun, that making revolution was the one thing which gave them a purpose in life; and now they have been told to stop it.

When it is remembered that 65 per cent of the population of China is under the age of 30 – that is, something like 650 million Chinese – then imagine the scale of the problem of those two categories of casualties of the Cultural Revolution: the victims and those who were embittered by their inability to go on with it.

Any great political upheaval breaks bones in the society which goes through that upheaval. One way of describing the history of France in the past 200 years is to say that the repeated political upheavals which started with the French Revolution and continued at intervals throughout the first two-thirds of the nineteenth century left behind a series of fractures in the bone structure of French society, each of which took a generation or more to heal. Now consider China. As a result of the experiences of the original Communist Revolution in 1949, followed by the Cultural Revolution in 1966 and then by the counter-revolution of Deng, the body politic of China is scarred by bone fractures in almost all its limbs. It will take a long time for them to heal.

ECONOMIC DIFFICULTIES

The unsolved economic problem is, in part, endemic to China itself, whatever government, regime or system runs it.

There are certain to be appalling problems for any country with a population of a billion people alive, not solved by the fact that China is an apparently very large country. In fact, the arable area of China is relatively small. The further west one proceeds into China the more one runs into either mountains – the highest mountains in the world – or into high upland steppes on which little can grow.

The arable area of China consists of a strip of land, perhaps 300 miles at its narrower parts and perhaps 600 miles wide at its furthest reaches. China has less than half of India's arable land, for a population far greater. China has less arable land than the countries of the European Community. It has one-seventh of the arable land of the United States.

It uses these extremely limited agricultural resources brilliantly. In the eastern part of China, where most of the food grows, an initial impression is that nothing else can be done with this land to make it more productive. There is hardly a wasted inch. The land up to every house is cultivated, cropped and tended.

There is an almost park-like appearance, because everything is kept in such beautiful order. The Chinese record in irrigation is first-class. The Chinese record in multiple-cropping is becoming first-class. The excellently irrigated and terraced fields of eastern China show that China is not far from the limits of what it can grow. There may be some prospect of improvement ahead, but there is not a great deal. That is the problem endemic to China itself.

The answer might seem to be: 'Very well, if we cannot do much more with agriculture, let us turn to industry.' Here we come to the part of the Chinese economic problem which is the weakness of the system, not just of being Chinese. The centralised command-structure of the Chinese economic system has precisely the same rigidity and bureaucracies which can be found in the Soviet Union. Under such a system, instructions flow from the planning structure at the top to the factories, telling them how much to produce, what to produce, at what prices they should sell it, what wages they should pay to their workers, where they should find their investment funds and what they could do with them. Virtually nothing is left to initiative or flexibility at the level of the factory itself. In this respect China has been, and to a large extent still is, very like Russia.

Manifestly, this was not working, even before the Cultural Revolution; and when the Cultural Revolution added to the rigidities of the central planning system its own special cultural revolutionary belief that what would really inspire people to work hard was revolutionary zeal – and three hours a day of political lectures in order to work up that revolutionary zeal – the inevitable happened: a decrepit economy became even more decrepit. I remember going to a machine tool factory just outside Canton in 1977 and seeing one stunning piece of visual evidence of the slovenliness which this system had produced. We came out of one of the main workshops and there on the ground, sitting in the snow outside the workshop, were great piles of half-made machines obviously unfit to send anywhere. They had simply been piled into heaps on either side of the exit from the workshop. I turned to the manager of the factory and said: 'What are these lumps of iron doing here? What are these things?' The translator translated it to him. I though I saw a jump of embarrassment in the manager's eye. He replied in Chinese. The translator turned to us and said: 'The manager says we leave our machinery here, until it assumes its proper shape.'

This appalling inefficiency was recognised by the counter-revolutionaries, and from 1977 onwards they made an attempt to put it right. They raised farm prices in order to provide an incentive for the peasants to work (and 800 million Chinese

people live and work on the land). Having tried to give extr
incentives to these 800 million people on the land, they increased
wages for the industrial workers, partly to enable them to pay
the higher cost of food, but also to provide them with an incentive
of their own. They shifted their industrial priorities fairly
markedly from heavy industry – which was the most inefficient
part of the system – to consumer-goods industries, partly to
provide more consumer-goods for people to spend their extra
money on but also partly to provide the kind of exports which
China could sell abroad in order to be able to buy more of the
technological imports it needs.

Having done these two intelligent things, they relaxed central
controls in a quite marked fashion. They made it possible for
factories which exceeded certain norms of production to hold
back a portion of the extra profits they had made by this success
and use these profits either by distributing them in bonuses to
the most successful workers or, in some cases, in a very tentative
way, by investing the extra profits. Here perhaps, at last, was
the beginning of a flexibility which would bring the green shoots
of initiative breaking through the concrete. They also allowed
certain provinces to engage directly in foreign trade with the
outside world, which had hitherto been an unthinkable proposition. In a more limited way they even allowed foreign capital
to come into two or three areas on the coastline of China from
capitalists from Hong Kong and Taiwan.

At first this experiment in decentralisation and flexibility
produced some marked successes. In 1978, the first full year of
the new period under Deng, total output went up about 12 per
cent, and industrial output about 13.5 per cent. I have visited a
number of factories in China which have been given permission
to operate the system of holding back some of their profits for
bonuses and clearly it has been a great success. The fact that by
working better and harder you can get more money has increased
production by amounts varying from 10 to 25 per cent.

There was, therefore, at the end of 1978 and the beginning of
1979, a distinct sense of exhilaration in China. The counter-
revolution – a word the Chinese themselves would never dare to
use – seemed to be working. But then it started to go sour. It
turned out, first, that the undoubted successes of 1978 were in
part simply a recovery of production to something like normal
levels after the shambles of the Cultural Revolution: the mere

return to some kind of order and discipline accounted for a substantial part of the bounce-back of 1978.

Secondly, and much more seriously, some of the underlying weaknesses of the Chinese economic system began to make themselves felt. The weakness, for instance, of the transport system. There is a great shortage of transport in China. One steel pipe factory in Sichuan had great piles of pipes accumulated outside it simply because it was unable to find transport to move them to the rest of the country. Then there is the shortage of energy. The latest figure I have seen is that China's industry is working at only about 70 per cent of its capacity mainly because of a shortage of energy. Then there is the problem of officials and middle-level managers who simply do not understand what Deng and the reformists are trying to achieve – men who were appointed during Mao's time and the Cultural Revolution, and simply cannot understand the merits of flexibility and decentralisation which the new men are trying to impose upon them. Furthermore, China has run into the problem of inflation of six per cent, and a suggestion that in some cities it may be running as high as 18 per cent.

The effect of this disappointment, after the exhilaration of the first year or so of the reform programme, has been marked. In the spring of 1979 the frustrated reformists had to announce what they called a period of readjustment, by which they meant a period of reducing targets, which they forecast would last for three years. This period of readjustment has now been lengthened to five years. More worryingly, it has recently been announced – and I do not know how widespread this is – that the experiments in decentralisation are to be frozen. The problems that have shown up in the attempt to work out a more flexible structure, added to the underlying weaknesses of the economy, have brought to at least a temporary halt this most hopeful development.

I am not suggesting that failure is general in the Chinese economy. It is not. Consumer industry production in 1980 according to some figures, is said to have risen by 17.5 per cent. That is good by any standards. There are other success stories. But in general the lesson to be learnt from the attempt to recover from the chaos of the Cultural Revolution is that China has an enormously long way to go before its economy will be working at anything like adequate efficiency.

THE PROBLEM OF IDENTITY

This was very important during Chairman Mao's time. China seemed to be, and indeed was in many respects, different from the Soviet Union. It was different from Russia partly in that it gave far more attention and emphasis to the agricultural sector of life. As I said earlier, 80 per cent of the population still works and lives on the land. This was not the experience of Stalin's Russia or, indeed, of capitalist Europe in the nineteenth century, both of which set out to base their economics on industry and to draw people off the land in order to work in industry. China took a deliberate decision not to go that way but to keep most of its population based on the land, with village industries in the communes. That was, I think, a very sound decision, and that has not been fundamentally changed by the new men.

But the main thing which distinguished China from Russia in the period of Chairman Mao was the idea of permanent or repeated revolution, a revolution a generation, the idea of calling out the Red Guards to cleanse the party from within. If there is one thing that is certain about China under its present leadership it is that this has been abandoned. It has been dismissed as a total disaster. That leaves China looking not very different from the Soviet Union – not a different kind of communist power. After all, it is political structure that counts, and the political structure of China is, in terms of party organisation and government system, really not very different from that of the Soviet Union. The trial of Mrs Mao has reminded us of episodes in Soviet history which we would rather have forgotten.

Even in matters of foreign policy, China has dropped its rather idiosyncratic assertions of the Mao period. It used to claim that the world was divided into three groups of countries: the Superpowers, meaning Russia and America; the medium-sized developed countries; and the rest, the undeveloped countries, of which China naturally claimed the leadership. Even this claim to be different has now been diluted.

There are still major differences between Russia and Deng's China. There is still scope in China for some dissent and questioning of what the government does: not very much, but maybe a little more than there is in the Soviet Union. There is that pregnant slogan of Deng's which, if he carries it through, could in the end bring real change to China – the pragmatist slogan that 'Experience is the test of truth'. There is also something racial. A Japanese friend once said to me: 'When I look at the Russians, I see something heavy and dark. When I look at the Chinese, I see something light.' There is if you will forgive an element of romanticism, a surviving charm in China which I do not find when I go to the Soviet world. There are still these differences. But I do not think they are enough for the Chinese to claim to be something distinctive from Russia, an alternative centre of ideological power.

So is China an international power? In terms of military weapons, the most obvious test, no. It has nuclear weapons, but nuclear weapons which it would find difficult to use in almost any circumstances except retaliating against a nuclear attack by Russia. Its non-nuclear forces are elderly, decrepit and lacking in capability.

Is it an international power in economic terms? Japan has shown that a country can be an international economic power without being militarily strong. But in the case of China, surely, on the evidence of this analysis of its economy, no, it is not an international power.

It is not an international power if political stability is the test because if I am right in my analysis we cannot claim political stability for China until it has worked out the unresolved problems of the Cultural Revolution. Nor is it an international power in the sense of having a really distinctive ideology; not any longer.

I think I would claim for China two things. First, it can be a centre of attention, even a centre of authority, for those Marxist–Leninist states that wish to distinguish themselves from the Soviet Union. There are some, but there are not very many of them. If China is relying upon being, as it were, the leader of the opposition inside the communist world, it is going to find itself leading a rather small minority. Second, it does have the power – in sheer weight of numbers and even, perhaps, in its limited military capacity – to overawe some of its small neighbours. Unless, that is, those small neighbours can find an alternative and even more powerful protector, in Russia, in America, in Vietnam, or even in Japan. In 1979 China engaged in a war with Vietnam. The best that can be said of that war from China's point of view is that it was a draw; some people would even argue that the Vietnamese beat China.

Only in one other sense do I think that China can claim the right to the title of real power. That is the fact that it is an indigestible country. It is just too big, in square miles and numbers of people, to be overrun and held down by any invader. No invader, I think, can believe that he could occupy China and continue to control it indefinitely. In that sense there may be indeed only three indigestible countries in the world: the Soviet Union, China and the United States. In that extremely limited sense I am willing to grant China the status of a Superpower. In the other more modest ways that I have discussed, it could be regarded as an international power. But in no other. China's power is limited first by the problems innate in being China, but second, and more important, by the limitations created by the mistakes of the past 30 years, and above all by the disaster of the Cultural Revolution.

6 Japan's Foreign and Security Policies

BRIGADIER KENNETH HUNT

This chapter sets out to describe Japan's foreign and security policies as they are today and to offer some thoughts on the way in which they may develop in the future. It comments in passing on the nature of Japanese power, political, economic and military. It makes an attempt to capture something of the rather special flavour of the debate in Japan.

It has become commonplace that there are political, perhaps even cultural barriers to any wider security role for Japan, or to an acceleration of defence programmes. When Prime Minister Nakasone took office in November 1982, the impact that he made internationally through his willingness to speak out on defence matters – uncharacteristic of Japanese statesmen – led many to believe that the barriers might soon be lowered. In time, some of them may be, but so far the Prime Minister's rhetoric has tended to outrun reality. The trend line of slow, incremental growth targets set almost a decade ago has not been broken. A consensus behind greater defence efforts has not yet appeared and until it is formed, no significant change is likely. In the meantime, however, there is growing awareness of the need for Japan to play a larger part in safeguarding its foreign policy interests and growing confidence in its ability to do so, though not militarily.

SOME HISTORY

Japan's present policies and attitudes have largely been formed by the events of the last half-century and it is necessary to recapitulate some of them, to give perspective for judgements about the future.

Before World War II, Japan was an important military power, regionally dominant because China was weak and the Soviet Union was preoccupied with Europe. It had annexed Formosa (Taiwan) and Korea around the turn of the century and in the 1930s took over Manchuria and invaded North China. During the war, under military leadership, it spread throughout East Asia. It was then disastrously beaten; the atomic bombs were dropped; the military was utterly discredited, which has had its effects on policies ever since. Japan's activities in Asia in the 1920s, 1930s and 1940s represent a mortgage on the past, which is still being repaid.

In 1945 Japan was occupied and a Constitution was imposed which outlawed armed force. In 1949 the communists attained power in China and Asia became polarised between East and West. Occupied Japan was automatically in the Western camp. In 1952 the Occupation ended, Japan became independent and concluded Peace and Security Treaties with the United States. From that point on the link with the United States became the centrepiece of Japanese foreign and security policy. It still is. For Japan, the Security Treaty provided obvious advantages: the US Navy ensured the freedom of the seas on which the growing Japanese trade depended, and US forces in the Pacific, South Korea and Taiwan maintained regional stability. Japan's external defence, conventional and nuclear, was found by the United States, which in return obtained forward bases in the Japanese islands and an important political and trading partner. So there was mutual interest, which has made the link durable. Japan left political and security problems to the United States, which wanted to exercise leadership anyway, and got on with the business of earning its living. It separated economics from politics.

For some twenty years, Japan lived in this cocoon, sheltered from the world outside and prospering remarkably. Defence was politically a taboo subject; the memory of the military failures and their costs were fresh. The Self-Defense Forces, which had their origins in a police force set up by the Occupation authorities for internal security purposes during the Korean War, operated under severe political constraints. They existed despite the Constitution primarily because Japan, when it became a member of the United Nations in 1956, claimed the right to self-defence under the UN Charter. But they were small and were responsible only for the direct defence of Japan itself, leaving all else to US forces under the provisions of the Security Treaty. They were permitted strictly defensive weapons only.

Then came a series of jolts to Japan's feeling of security. In 1971, President Nixon reversed US policy towards China with no warning to Japan, and instituted protectionist measures against Japanese goods. In 1973 the Arab oil embargo reminded Japan acutely of its vulnerability to external supplies of energy and raw materials. In 1975, US forces having left Vietnam, Saigon fell; Japan agonised over a possible loss of American interest in East Asia, lent force by President Carter's proposal in 1976–77 to withdraw US ground forces from South Korea. In 1978, Vietnam invaded Cambodia, actively helped by the Soviet Union, and then in 1979–80 came the invasion of Afghanistan and the Iran–Iraq War, both highlighting the instability of the region on which Japan depended for most of its energy. These last two events and the earlier revolution in Iran had the effect of drawing US forces away from the Pacific to the Middle East, at a time when the Soviet military presence in East Asia was steadily growing.

All of these developments were a reminder that Japan had little influence over its international environment. While it had outgrown its earlier economic dependence on the United States, it was still dependent on it for its security and for the protection of its interests – and it had become apparent that these might not always be identical with those of Washington. It was also plain that US forces were now stretched and no longer able to dominate the Pacific as they once could.

THE REGIONAL CONTEXT

For many Japanese the ideal foreign policy would be one which adopted a political position equidistant between those of the three great powers in Asia: China, the Soviet Union and the United States, so as to have complete freedom of manoeuvre. While Japan is in fact tied closely to the United States, it has tried over the years to keep working relationships with China and Moscow. The links with China are now good but those with Moscow are little better than cool.

China has long exercised a cultural pull in Japan and when American policy towards China changed in 1971, Japan, now free to change its own stance, hastened to do this. However, it took some seven years before a Peace Treaty was signed in August 1978, because China wanted this to record Japan's opposition to Soviet hegemony. Japan was reluctant to agree to this; while it wanted good relations with China it did not want to antagonise the Soviet Union in the process. Tokyo did not see the Treaty in the same political and strategic light as Beijing, and when eventually it signed a document that largely met Chinese wishes, Japan assured the Soviet Union that it was not directed against anyone.

But the Soviet Union thought it was and saw Japan as shifting its weight into the Chinese scale – which was in part true. When Washington normalised relations with China shortly afterwards, in early 1979, Moscow spoke of a US–Japan–China alliance against the Soviet Union.

Though Japan certainly had begun to place emphasis on links with China, it would have been ready to reach a Peace Treaty with the Soviet Union as well. There was, however, an impediment in the way of this, a Soviet unwillingness to discuss the return of the four Northern Islands occupied by the Soviet Union since World War II but claimed by Japan as its own. Soviet policy towards Japan, always clumsy and overbearing, became distinctly cool in the wake of the Treaty with China. Soviet military activity in the region took on a somewhat demonstrative air, including the very pointed step of putting a strong military force into the Islands, which had long been only lightly manned. Moscow could have had strategic reasons for this deployment, to help safeguard one of the exits from the Sea of Okhotsk, an operating area for Soviet missile-submarines, but it caused great resentment in Japan. Popular feeling against the Soviet Union grew. The steady growth of Soviet military strength in East Asia coupled with Soviet actions in Afghanistan and in support of Vietnam in Cambodia, all led to a chilly climate of relations. The slow growth of Japanese public support for an increase in defence spending owes as much to the abrasive nature of Soviet policies as to any other factors.

THE ECONOMY AND FOREIGN POLICY

Japan had, of course, some military strength of its own but this was dwarfed by that of the Soviet Union and China (albeit of a somewhat different kind) and was much smaller than that of its two Korean neighbours. So it was in no practical sense a military power in the Far East, let alone in the world outside. And this despite its resources. It had simply not chosen to try to match its military power to its economic might.

Of this there can be no doubt. Japan's GNP had grown enormously, to become the second largest in the non-communist world. In 1960 its share of world GNP was three per cent, in 1980 ten per cent. It had a huge home market, so that exports were only around 13 per cent of GNP, around half the proportion for West Germany. But it needed to export to pay for raw materials and energy imports, since it had almost none of its own. As the economy grew, so did the vulnerability to external supplies. Japan traded hard internationally (as Japanese do at home, being intensely competitive) and built up large trade surpluses, notably with the United States, where it met protectionist barriers as a result.

The word 'linkage' appeared. Japan was widely regarded by Americans, particularly in sections of Congress, as enjoying a 'free ride' in defence. While the United States was spending around seven per cent of GNP ($846 per capita) on defence, the Japanese level was just less than one per cent ($87 per capita). Japan was thought to be putting resources into industry instead, thus gaining advantage over American competitors. It was benefiting from the international stability ensured by the United States but not contributing fairly to the costs involved. There were pressures for Japan to spend more on defence and to open up its markets more, points which will be returned to later.

Japan trades widely in Asia and its economy is a motor for other vigorous economies in the region: South Korea, Taiwan, Hong Kong, the ASEAN countries. It is the principal supplier of capital to China and is thus important to that country's modernisation. The bulk of Japan's economic aid goes to Asia. All this gives Japan some influence, though its diplomatic leverage may depend on the nature of the trading balance and geopolitical considerations. Where countries provide the raw materials Japan wants – Indonesia and Malaysia, for example –

the strength can be on their side to some extent, Japan being the *demandeur*. Japan's need for shipping routes through the Malacca and Singapore Straits calls for careful diplomacy and good relations. But, of course, Japan has important things to offer, such as technology, training, capital and very acceptable goods, plus a very large though not very welcoming market – the United States is far from being alone in its complaints about the difficulty of exporting to Japan anything other than raw materials or energy.

Japan's economic power has much the same strengths and weaknesses elsewhere in the world. In the Middle East, the fact that some 65 per cent of Japan's oil comes from there makes sensitive diplomacy necessary, the more so since that oil is from both sides of the Gulf. In Africa and Latin America, both suppliers of raw materials and markets for Japanese goods, Japan treads warily. Here it is important to make a point of Tokyo's reluctance to get involved in political problems. The Japanese are not internationally minded – other than as traders. Japan is a strongly ethnocentric society, long cut off from the world and still more so than other major countries. Japanese governments since the war have shied away from international entanglements, which had only seemed to bring misfortune; for 30 years or so they let the United States deal with difficult external problems and themselves kept a low posture. This suited Washington since Japan thus had no policy of its own and so was a biddable partner. But this suits Tokyo no longer if Japanese interests suffer. After the oil embargo of 1973, Japan saw the need to be on good terms with Arab oil producers and switched from a policy of favouring Israel because the United States did. Policy has since become less passive.

Japan is, however, still heavily reliant on good relations with the United States, on which it depends for its security and which is its largest market – 29 per cent as compared with some 16 per cent for South-East Asia and around 13 per cent for the European Community. For these relations it has to pay a certain price, just as Europe does, similarly dependent for its defence. Accordingly, the present Japanese Prime Minister, Nakasone Yasuhiro, when taking office in November 1982, made a visit to Washington one of his first tasks, to repair links that had become rather strained, not least by trading frictions. Like his predecessors, he went bearing gifts: some measures to open the Japanese market a little and a long-delayed agreement to permit transfer of Japanese military technology to the United States, the usual coupling of items to meet complaints about trade imbalances and Japanese reluctance to do more about defence. He stressed that Japan was an ally (a touchy issue in Japan, discussed later); he recognised the need for greater defence efforts and generally gave the impression that from now on things would be better. At the Williamsburg Summit in May 1983 he went so far as to support the NATO position on INF negotiations – the first time a Japanese Prime Minister had ever spoken on a security issue outside the realms of the US–Japan Security Treaty. This was a brave political step, since support for the possible deployment of nuclear weapons is a sensitive subject in Japan, even if the weapons were to be in Europe. His position was sound enough, since NATO was contending that negotiations should cover the Soviet SS-20 missiles in Asia as well as those in Europe; it suited Japan that NATO should carry the burden of negotiating about the Asian SS-20 rather than that it should get involved in nuclear negotiations itself. The problem has by no means gone away, however; Tokyo may yet have to take a view on US nuclear weapons in Asia as well.

CHANGE

Since the present nature of Japan's external and security policies is neither wholly satisfactory to Tokyo nor Washington, some change seems likely over the years. The present position is, however, much more tolerable to Japan than to the United States, certainly as far as trade and security are concerned, and the constraints on rapid movement are deeply embedded in the Japanese political and social system. When there is pressure from outside, as for example from the US Congress on trade, Japan may make concessions that alter policy a little. But these are inevitably made at the cost of domestic political interests and so only with reluctance and slowly. It is often a case of too little and too late, so that political goodwill is unduly forfeited. Some outside developments would produce change, perhaps of a dramatic sort. If some quite evident and direct threat to Japan's own security were to appear, the Japanese people could be galvanised into making military efforts that at present they do not see as warranted and which have bitter historical associations. There is no suggestion of this at the moment, since nobody feels threatened, however much there may be an awareness of an unfriendly Soviet military presence in the region. Or if the United States decided to draw back from East Asia and keep no forces forward at all, Japan would be faced with a problem of defence that it does not at present have. It could decide to build up its armed strength materially, or to depend on diplomacy instead. While such an American withdrawal is unlikely, Japanese foreign policy must always guard against it.

There is little doubt that the idea that Japan will have to do more for its own security is slowly gaining wider acceptance in the country. The Prime Minister is ahead of public opinion on the issue and unlikely to bring the rapid change sometimes expected of him outside Japan. Nonetheless he has been changing the terms of the debate a little; defence is no longer the taboo issue that it once was and defence appropriations that are slightly higher do not have to be fought through against quite the opposition that there was in the past. Public hostility to the Self-Defense Forces, once a feature of Japanese life, has all but gone except on the political left. But there are still limits and still not many votes in defence. On defence spending, strong elements in the governing Liberal Democratic Party still feel that enough should be done to keep the United States reasonably quiet, but not much more. Certainly, nobody wants to build up the Japanese forces so that they can take over roles from US forces, so enabling them to sail away to the Indian Ocean. Asian neighbours are at one on this: when they sometimes make noises about a possible resurgence of Japanese militarism – of which they have bitter memories – their immediate concern is with a resulting diminution of the US military presence in the Western Pacific.

There is a consensus behind an incremental growth in defence spending, which looks like being at the rate of four and a half per cent in real terms in the current year, marginally above the rate of increase in each of the three previous years. This compares favourably with the NATO target of three per cent annual growth – which is rarely met – but it is from a relatively low base. Expenditure is likely to be just inside one per cent of GNP, a limit set by the Cabinet in 1976 in order to get a long-range defence programme through the Diet. The programme is, however, running behind and higher spending would be needed to achieve its goals in FY 1987, which is when the United States has said it is expecting them to be achieved. This extra is not likely to be found; as it is, defence and foreign aid are the only two items in the national budget which have been allowed to rise at all, an indication of the Prime Minister's willingness to give priority to defence. But even the present rate of growth may burst the one per cent barrier quite soon – an important threshold politically, which could use up some political capital at a time when social spending is having to give way.

There is another problem, less obvious than that of defence spending: the nature of Japan's role. Washington regards Japan as an ally and Nakasone used the term when in Washington. His predecessor, Suzuki, used it too, but then had to back away from it on his return to Japan. The issue has arisen because the US–Japan Security Treaty makes the United States responsible for defending Japan but places no responsibilities on Japan. Japan interprets its Constitution as entitling it to defend itself when directly attacked but not to be a member of any collective defence arrangement which contains the obligation to take up arms in a common cause. So formally, Japan can cooperate with the United States if Japan is attacked, but not in any other conflict. It is thus only a limited ally. Furthermore the 1976 defence programme provides for forces designed only for this limited purpose and not for anything wider. Washington thus faces a double disappointment: having Japan fail to meet the goals on time; and to have forces for strictly limited purposes. Over time this limitation may disappear. If war broke out in East Asia, it might be removed anyway, as Japanese interests were seen to be threatened. But for the moment the constraint is there and the Japanese forces have in any case a long way to go before they are adequate for their more limited tasks.

There are well-publicised weaknesses in the Self-Defense Forces and in their sustainability, which the long-term pro-gramme is endeavouring to put right, using the incremental growth in spending. In the last year or two, the American pressure for higher defence spending has been somewhat muted and greater emphasis has been placed on measures which are not particularly costly, those designed to enable US and Japanese forces to work better together. Though the Security Treaty is almost exactly as old as NATO, US and Japanese forces have nothing like the ability to work together as do those in Europe. There are scant arrangements for joint 'allied' control and only in the last year or two have the US and Japanese forces begun to train together with any regularity. It must be said that the Self-Defense Forces have not worked with each other either; there is no joint headquarters to command the three Japanese services; distrust of the military was such that no joint command could be set up lest it should give them too much power. Historically understandable but militarily ridiculous, this attitude is also in process of change – but slowly.

So there is forward movement. This is partly because of the changing international environment – not least Soviet activities – partly through American pressure for Japan to play a greater part in defence. This pressure has been noticeably less since Nakasone took office, perhaps because Washington does not want to damage his domestic political position. Washington does have the leverage to force things along but knows that it is better to use this sensitively. The Japanese want policy to be made in Tokyo. There are limits to the speed with which even a strong politician can bring about change, since in Japan he must first create a consensus. And Japanese politicians are not strong in the sense that Western ones can be, able to make things happen quickly. Government in Japan is a balance of power in effect, between politicians, business and bureaucrats, each needing to be accommodated before acceptable policy emerges. In the meantime, Nakasone has taken firm steps to gain the confidence of Washington and of the President, with whom he has developed a remarkable and valuable personal relationship.

The links with the United States are the basis of Japan's external policies, foreign, security and economic. Many of these policies are designed by bureaucrats, even made by them. The younger generation of these gifted and powerful officials wants to see policies clearly serving Japanese interests and to see Japanese political initiatives that make use of economic strength. They are much more international in outlook than the politicians. Many would be content – some even anxious – to see Japan militarily stronger, though firmly within the context of the security ties with the United States.

Realism imposes certain limits though. Japan lives next to two large communist powers, one a difficult, unyielding Superpower, the other with massive manpower and not wholly predictable

---

behaviour. Japan could not match their military capabilities and has no wish or intention to acquire nuclear weapons to counter theirs, even if this were possible. The alliance with the United States is at once the most sensible way in which to ensure Japan's security, perhaps on a more equal footing than now. Japan's problem is how to acquire political strength to match its economic preponderance. It is not feasible to attempt to ensure access to raw materials and energy by military means, given the huge distances involved and the diversity of the sources, and so Japan must rest on diplomatic efforts and on the international order largely kept by the United States and which it does so little to sustain itself. Japan could do more and is indeed slowly assuming a greater international role, though not yet the international responsibilities that other developed nations have long carried. But when Japan's own interests are directly affected, Tokyo does act, quickly though not always boldly. Japan is still far from being internationalist in outlook. Until it is, the extent of its influence must be limited. There will be change, but Japan's recent history suggests that this will come only slowly in the absence of powerful external pressures.

7 Australia's Outlook on Asia

PHILIP TOWLE

For a quarter of a century Australian politicians and commentators regarded China as the main threat to stability in Asia. In 1965 a leading Australian academic, Coral Bell, commented that 'attitudes towards China may justly be regarded as the central or catalytic element in Australia's diplomatic alignments since 1949'. It was primarily against the Chinese that Australian forces had fought alongside other UN troops in Korea and during the 1960s it was against North Vietnam and the Viet Cong – which were then regarded as Chinese agents – that the Australians fought in Indochina. When President Sukarno dominated Indonesia, Australia's closest Asian neighbour, many believed it to be in danger of falling under Chinese influence. Yet for the last decade and more, Australians have been adapting to a situation in which relations between China and the West have improved dramatically, in which China is perceived as an agent of stability rather than of discord, and in which a striking growth of Soviet naval power in Asia has focused Western concerns on Vladivostok and Cam Ranh Bay rather than Beijing.

The number of days spent by Soviet warships in the Pacific rose from a mere 200 in 1956 to 11,800 in 1980 and from zero in the Indian Ocean in 1956 to 11,800 24 years later. These changes caused a great deal of concern in Australia and in the West in general. They indicated that the Soviet Union had become a Superpower with a global reach. The expansion of the Soviet fleet gave the Kremlin the capability to intervene in peacetime in areas where it was previously impotent. There were fears in Australia that it might even begin to take an interest in the Pacific Islands, particularly in the event of political unrest or disturbance. In a general East–West war, the main purpose of the Soviet Fleet would be to prevent US reinforcements from reaching Western Europe. In Asia it could also be employed to seize parts of Northern Japan to ensure unimpeded egress from Vladivostok. In such a conflict, Australia would find itself fighting on the side of a world-wide coalition; an experience familiar from the two world wars. But the outcome would be decided ultimately by trials of strength in which Australian power would be peripheral and marginal.

Some Australians have argued that the country should isolate itself from such dangers by breaking with the Western coalition. Links with the USA have been built up since 1942 and were solidified by the ANZUS alliance in 1951. The most sensitive aspect of the American relationship is the location on Australian soil of intelligence-gathering posts. There is a communications facility at North West Cape which is said to be able to transmit messages to US SSBNs. In the interior there are further posts at Pine Gap and Nurrungar which are involved in space tracking and communications. There have always been Australians who have regarded these facilities as a derogation of the country's sovereignty and the terms under which they are maintained were renegotiated by the Whitlam government in the 1970s. The controversy has, however, grown as the image of the US has changed because of the Vietnam war and as East–West relations have deteriorated in the 1980s. Many fear that Australia might be dragged into a war against its wishes and the Hawke government has admitted that the posts on Australian territory might be prime targets in a nuclear war. Defenders of the US links argue that such facilities play a part in maintaining the strategic balance and in verification of Strategic Arms Limitations Agreements. They are also deemed to be a small price to pay for US friendship and alliance commitment.

For the foreseeable future these pro-American views appear likely to prevail but Australians still feel the need to be able to protect themselves against lesser threats in the Asian region. The practical defence debate in Canberra turns on how much protection is necessary against such contingencies. The country has a long tradition of spending little on defence in peacetime and then rearming rapidly in a crisis. Australia does not manufacture major items of military equipment such as main battle tanks and combat aircraft and could only do so at high unit cost. In an emergency, extra weapons would have to be purchased abroad and procurement times would depend upon the other demands made on the industries of the US and Europe. Furthermore, training times have become longer as weapons have become more complicated. Hence, the citizen armies which Australia conjured out of the ground in two world wars might be more difficult to create. On the other hand, notice of threat is anticipated. Australian defence assessments point out that 'in the unlikely event that other countries developed motive or intent to launch a major military force against Australia, the substantial forces needed would take many years to develop, even with massive external assistance'.

Geography is the country's main ally in this respect. An amphibious attack on Australia would be extremely hazardous even for the strongest maritime powers. The country's six Oberon class submarines, its 24 F-III fighter-bombers and its 53 Mirage III aircraft would make it essential for an attacking force to deploy both aircraft carriers and anti-submarine frigates. Furthermore, even if it were possible to protect such a force and to land troops, there are few areas in Australia where a landing could have a major military effect or even support itself. Only the capture of one of the main cities would give it an effective foothold. Thus most Australian commentators regard minor raids as a more probable threat than a substantial seaborne invasion, particularly as such raids could be expected by air as
• well as by sea. According to Dr T. B. Millar, 'the only reason that we have the F-IIIs is that fourteen years ago Indonesia confronted Malaya in a tiny war and sent an occasional Soviet-supplied bomber cruising over an undefended and largely unaware North. In an excess of alarm at what this might mean at the 1963 election, the Menzies government ordered the F-III off the drawing board.' The most serious threat could come from bombers based in Indonesia were it again to become hostile but attacks could come also from the Asian mainland. Australian defence policy has to take account of such a prospect.

Australia spends about 3.1 per cent of gross national product on defence, compared with 10.2 per cent by North Korea, 7.6 per cent spent by South Korea, 8 per cent by Malaysia but only 3.9 per cent by Thailand and 2.2 per cent by the Philippines. Moreover the size of Australia's forces contrasts strongly with those of most of its neighbours. Australia's armed forces are small and professional. They number about 72,000 men. Indonesia has four times as many under arms, Vietnam 14 times as many, and China 60 times as many. Of these three countries Australians are probably most concerned currently about Vietnam because of its confrontation with the ASEAN states and about Indonesia because of its proximity to Australia itself. Vietnam, however, is fully occupied with a guerrilla war in Kampuchea and with its frontier skirmishes with China. Indonesia could only become a possible threat once more if Canberra handled its relations with Jakarta extremely badly, or if relations between Indonesia and Papua New Guinea deteriorated out of hand but even then, Indonesia's limited military capability would serve as a constraint.

AUSTRALIA AND ITS NEIGHBOURS

The most dramatic changes took place in Australia's policy towards Asia in the 1970s with the election of the first Labour government for two decades. Many of the new policies introduced by the Prime Minister, Gough Whitlam, have endured to this day. The government reduced Australia's military presence in Asia, recognised the People's Republic of China, and accepted the need to improve relations with other Asian states. It tried to present a more 'liberal' image by announcing changes in Australia's immigration laws to admit more non-whites, by reducing sporting links with South Africa and by advancing the country's main colony, Papua New Guinea, towards independence. Australia's defence links with the US were re-examined and some support was given to the idea of establishing a nuclear weapon free zone in the Pacific and a Peace Zone in the Indian Ocean. Visiting Australia in 1973 Lord Chalfont commented 'they have accepted the realities of their geographic situation and its ... implications'.

Some of the Whitlam government's changes had been forced upon it by outside events. Britain had announced its intention of withdrawing forces from East of Suez by the early 1970s. The US was also reducing its commitment to Asia in general and Vietnam in particular. In his 'Guam' doctrine of July 1969 and his report to Congress on foreign policy in February 1970 President Nixon made clear his administration's determination that the US should bear a smaller share of the burden of defending the non-communist world, especially in Asia. The war in Vietnam in particular was to be fought with Vietnamese rather than primarily American troops.

Australia had been more closely involved in Vietnam than any other non-Asian power except the US. As Roy Jenkins put it at the time, Australia had 'accepted the move away from the filial relationship with London but found instead an ill-timed role as L. B. Johnson's favourite nephew when not only was the uncle close to political death (without any bequests to make) but 25 years of American leadership was about to crumble before the eyes of the world'. Australian forces served in Vietnam from 1965 to 1971 and an Australian military advisory team was there from 1962 to 1972. The commitment resulted in an increase in the size of the armed forces from about 46,000 in 1960–61 to 87,000 in 1969–70. The maximum number of Australians serving there at any time was only about 8,000 but the campaign had a considerable impact on Australian politics. Anti-war demonstrations took place just as they did in most Western states and there were fears in Australia that relations with other Asian countries would be damaged. As Bruce Miller, the Professor of International Relations in Canberra put it in 1967, 'the longer the war goes on, the more concern there is about possible Australian unpopularity in Asia at large'.

If the Vietnam war shook Australian politics and contributed to Gough Whitlam's election victory, most Australians were impressed by the way that their forces had operated. *The Canberra Times* commented in January 1980, 'the Australians ... had generally a good reputation in Vietnam. During my time there I was impressed with the high level of civil aid undertaken by the Task Force in Phouc Toy province for example, health programmes, technical farming advice, building etc. The Viet Cong had wisely chosen other provinces to disrupt after having found the Australians too serious in their operations particularly after the battle of Long Tan in August 1966.' On the other hand, Australians 'who had contact with the Americans were not very impressed .... Respect among the Australians for the American war effort at the operational level was often low.'

After the end of the Vietnam War and with the evident split between China and Vietnam, many Australians began to question the whole traditional forward strategy of conducting operations in Asia in order to protect the homeland. Should not defences be withdrawn from Singapore and Malaysia and defence planning concentrate on threats to Australia itself? Since such a move would have coincided with Britain's withdrawal, it would have been extremely unpopular in the South-East Asian countries involved. Moreover, in 1971 a five-power defence agreement had been signed by Malaysia, Singapore, New Zealand, Britain and Australia. Under its terms, Australia was to maintain two squadrons of Mirage III aircraft at Butterworth in northern Malaya. Only in 1983 was one of these withdrawn; the other will follow between 1986 and 1988. The Australian government would have liked to avoid replacing them with RAAF F/A-18s because of the cost of servicing these more advanced aircraft in Malaya. However, under pressure from the Malaysian and Singapore governments, it has agreed to keep one squadron a year at Butterworth for a minimum of 16 weeks a year from 1988. Despite their anxieties about Asia, Australians are by no means always unwelcome there.

For their part, Australians have to learn to live with their Asian neighbours whatever policies they follow. This has been well illustrated by the issue of East Timor. Following the overthrow of the conservative Portuguese government in 1974, chaos descended on this Asian colony in the following year. In December 1975 Indonesian forces annexed the territory, partly out of fear that a Marxist government under Fretilin (Revolutionary Front for the Liberation of East Timor) might consolidate its power. The population, or a significant part of it, resisted the Indonesians but was brutally crushed. There were reports that 100,000 people might have died out of a population of 670,000. The territory was formally incorporated into Indonesia in July 1976. It is believed that the Australian government initially encouraged the Indonesians to invade but there are politicians in both the Liberal and especially the Labour Party who maintain that Canberra should have protested against the original seizure and denounced the subsequent repression. Australia, however, lacked the military power to intervene. Furthermore, good relations with Jakarta are more important to Australia than those with any other Asian capital and protests would simply have worsened relations without helping the inhabitants of East Timor.

Relations with Indonesia are sensitive because of the history of recent years and the weakness of Papua New Guinea. Australia opposed Indonesia over its claim to West Irian and backed Malaysia and Britain during the period of confrontation with Sukarno's government in the mid-1960s. Furthermore, Australia's colony of Papau New Guinea had a common frontier with Indonesia after August 1962. The colony became independent in 1975 but Canberra still feels a considerable responsibility for the security of its two and a half million people who are spread over 178,000 square miles. Instability either in Indonesia or in Papua New Guinea could threaten relations between Canberra and Jakarta. During 1984 there were reports that some 300 political refugees had fled across the frontier from Indonesia. Indonesian military aircraft intruded into Papua New Guinea and journalists were banned from the area. In the event relations were 'patched up' but the episode illustrated the sensitivity of the situation and the need for Canberra to avoid policies which might jeopardise the safety of its former colony.

Moreover, Australia has been caught up in the miniature Cold War between ASEAN and Vietnam. Before the Vietnamese invasion of Kampuchea in 1978 Canberra was planning to give aid to Vietnam partly, cynics might argue, to assuage the Australian conscience for the damage done during the Vietnam War. Subsequently, however, relations were strained and the ASEAN states have argued that they should not be improved until Vietnamese troops withdraw from Kampuchea. Some Australian commentators believe that this policy only pushes Hanoi further into Moscow's arms. Indeed the Hawke government has flirted with the idea of reversing the policy. In 1983, Australia refused to co-sponsor the annual ASEAN resolution on Kampuchea at the UN and the differences became public. Subsequently, Mr Hayden, the Foreign Minister, told Parliament 'there should be no iron curtain in this part of the world. The future of Australia lies in developing a mature and balanced set of relationships with its neighbours in South East Asia. Indochina is part of that neighbourhood.' Mr Hawke had already visited Vietnam and the Vietnamese Foreign Minister, Nguyen Co Thach, paid a visit to Australia in March 1984. The diplomatic isolation of Vietnam has been so great in recent years that Hanoi has warmly welcomed Australian overtures. Australians, unlike Americans, have been allowed to search for the graves of their war dead in Vietnam. But the Hawke government cannot go far down this road without alienating the ASEAN countries and ultimately they are more important to Australia than Vietnam.

If Australians have ethical and political doubts about the policies of nearby states, they are often extremely sensitive to 'moral' criticisms of their own policies. In June 1980 the *Canberra Times* reported that 'the UN General Assembly's committee on decolonisation is expected later this year to approve consideration of a reference which alleges mass discrimination against aborigines'. In the event such a reference did not materialise and, in the meantime, a great deal of attention has been devoted to reducing aboriginal grievances. More land has been assigned to them under the 1978 Land Rights Act. In November 1982, for example, the government of South Australia allocated 102,000 square kilometres to aborigines in the North West of the state so that 10 per cent of the state's entire territory is now owned by aborigines. They also own about 30 per cent of the Northern Territory. Nevertheless, apart from land ownership, there are other aboriginal grievances including lack of health provisions and lack of control over the mineral rights on land which they own. Medical standards are certainly lower for aborigines than for the rest of Australians. There has also been concern expressed that some aborigines have been harmed by nuclear weapons tests carried out by Britain in Australia 30 years ago. Over the next few years Australia will continue to be vulnerable to allegations at the UN that it is not treating its aborigines as equal citizens.

For Australians, immigration is as sensitive an issue as the treatment of aborigines. Up until the 1960s Australia's policies had been designed to encourage immigration from Europe and particularly from the British Isles. Nevertheless all laws actually discriminating against immigration by non-whites were removed from the statute books between 1957 and 1966, though without much publicity. In 1973, Mr Whitlam made it official and overt policy that there should be no discrimination on political or national grounds. But the issue still causes concern. The late Hedley Bull, formerly of the Australian National University, has argued that Australia would have to become even more welcoming to non-European immigrants if it were to come to terms with its Asian environment. In 1975, he wrote 'if what Australia seeks to make secure is the vestigial elements of white racism within its own society, the indefinite continuation of its

privileges in terms of wealth and consumption of resources ...
then threats to Australia's security ... may seem very likely
indeed .... Given the circumstances of its Asian environment
Australia has no prospect of surviving as the kind of society it is
now.' Yet most Australians would assign the highest priority to
maintaining their standard of living and to change only to the
extent that they wanted to change rather than to do so to meet
Asian demands. Tensions over the issue have increased since
1975 as refugees from Indochina have settled in Australia in
increasing numbers. In 1984, immigration again became a major
political issue with the government proposing to accept more
Asian immigrants and the Liberal opposition calling for a
balance between Asian and European immigrants. Members of
Parliament almost came to blows in the House of Representatives
and there have been suggestions that the issue would play an
increasing part in forthcoming elections.

OPPORTUNITIES

Australia's importance as an exporter of raw materials to Asia
and to the rest of the world will undoubtedly increase over time.
Political turmoil in Southern Africa could hasten the process but
the growth of the Asian economies should bring about the same
result in the long run. Coal exports in particular should rise as
world-wide resources of oil become more expensive to recover.
One international report in May 1980 suggested that Australian
coal exports might increase by at least a factor of four by the
end of the century, from 40 million tonnes in 1977 to between
160 and 200 million tonnes by the year 2000. A few months
earlier an Australian government minister had suggested that
the total might even reach 270 million tonnes. Subsequently, a
drastic reduction in energy consumption by the industrial powers
occurred but, once their economies start to expand again, this
trend should be reversed. As a stable, though strike-prone, source
of vital industrial raw materials Australia's position should
become even more important. But such dependence is mutual
and Australia's economy will be affected by political instability
or conflict in Asia.

Partly because of the fears of such conflict, uranium is a very
sensitive export. According to a 1978 estimate Australia has 20

per cent of world reserves of uranium, whilst another assessment puts the figure as high as 27 per cent. However, there is a strong lobby which opposes its export. Many argue that, even if Australian uranium is only used for peaceful purposes, no safe way has been found for storing the spent fuel from reactors. Moreover, certain Asian states, such as Taiwan or South Korea, might at some stage be tempted to use their nuclear capacity to produce atomic weapons – however much they may deny this at the moment. Supporters of exports argue that the waste problem can be solved and scientists at the Research School of Earth Sciences in Canberra have developed what they believe is an effective way of handling this problem. They would place radioactive materials in synthetic rocks which would last millions of years until the dangerous materials had decayed. The exporters also argue that the risk of nuclear weapons proliferation can be reduced by a combination of economic, political and legal measures. Because of this controversy, it was not clear when the new Labour government came to power in 1983 whether uranium exports would be allowed at all. Nevertheless, the decision was taken to allow them to continue and they are expected to be worth £1,934 million up to 1996.

Exports of other materials are less controversial and are increasing in importance. The world's largest diamond field is thought to lie near Lake Argyle in Western Australia. Some estimates suggest that it could yield between 25 and 30 million carats a year against a world production in 1982 of 45 million carats. In 1981 Australia also mined 16.2 tonnes of gold, making it the fourth largest producer in the West, whilst the state of Western Australia alone is thought to contain the largest iron reserves outside the Soviet Union, 35,000 million tonnes. For the moment however coal is Australia's most important export earner, worth £1,085 million in 1981 or 10.2 per cent of Australia's total exports and with Japan taking 70 per cent of this figure.

There is a three-way trade across the Pacific with Australia exporting coal, iron and other raw materials to Japan; Japan sending electronic equipment, cars and other consumer goods to the US and the Americans sending capital and heavy industrial products to Australia. The strong economic links with the US have their critics, particularly on the left of the Australian political spectrum, where there is a general feeling that foreign ownership of Australian industries is damaging to the country's prosperity in the long run and reduces its freedom of action. Yet Australia cannot be developed without foreign capital, given the technical and other problems involved in building roads and developing natural resources and industries. If foreign ownership of resources causes resentment, so from time to time does the importance of the trade with Japan. Memories of World War II have not entirely faded. Moreover the Japanese on their side are extremely critical of the frequency of strikes in Australia since these interrupt the steady flow of raw materials to their industries. They have planned to reduce their dependence on Australian steaming coal from 65 per cent to 42 per cent by 1990. Over the years some of these misunderstandings have been reduced but many remain and Australia will continue to be torn between its economic needs and national anxieties.

Australia's economic relations are less intimate with Asian states other than Japan. The main obstacle to strengthening such connections stems from the fact that Australian exports – raw materials and food – are produced by very few people because of the capital intensive methods used. Coal is mined on the 'strip mine' system using immense machines and few men. Wheat farming is equally capital intensive. The vast majority of Australians live in a small number of very large towns – Sydney, Melbourne, Perth, Adelaide. Their contact with the outback, with the vast empty farms or with the mines far away in the interior is often limited. They derive their incomes – £165 a week on average in 1982 – from industry and commerce. Yet with such wage levels and given Australian working practices, they cannot compete with the dynamic growth industries of the Asian continent. Governments have tried to foster relations with ASEAN but the process has not been easy. In 1974–75 for example, two per cent of Australia's exports went to Indonesia and only 0.2 per cent of its imports came from there. For trade with Singapore, the most industrially advanced of the ASEAN states, the figures were 2.4 per cent and 1.6 per cent, whilst Malaysia took 2.2 per cent of Australian exports and supplied 0.7 per cent of its imports. Even with the teeming millions of the People's Republic of China, Australian trade is not large. In 1974–75, 2.9 per cent of Australian exports went to China and one per cent of its imports came from there. Australian wheat has played an important role in helping Beijing avoid mass starvation after crop failures but the economic relationship is not a strong one. Australian imports from China and the rest of Asia could rise substantially if its tariffs were reduced. But Australian industry survives only because of such barriers. Thus, although there has been some liberalisation of Australian trade policy in recent years, it is unlikely that this process will go far enough to satisfy the Asian nations.

CONCLUSION

With the decline of the Chinese threat to Asian stability, the region has become a more complicated place for Australians. Japan, the former enemy, has become the second or third ranking world economic power with very close economic relations with Australia. South-East Asia is divided between ASEAN and the Vietnamese with their 'protectorates' over Laos and Kampuchea. In the duel over the political future of Kampuchea, the USSR is clearly aligned with Vietnam and China with ASEAN, whilst Chinese and Vietnamese forces have clashed bloodily across their common frontier. The US is still closely involved in Australian and Asian affairs but its economic, political and military salience is reduced and therefore Australians have to act to a greater extent on their own. In the 1950s and 1960s they were informed about Asian wars because they were often participants themselves; today it is the presence of refugees in Australia and other friendly neighbouring states which reminds them of the bitter and prolonged guerrilla wars in Kampuchea and East Timor. In military terms, then, Australia is more isolated from Asian conflicts but psychologically and economically it is more deeply involved in Asian affairs, while the increase in Australian diplomatic representation in Asia means that governments in Canberra are better informed about the region.

Opportunities for Canberra to improve relations with China and other Asian countries have increased but Australians find it difficult to comprehend the harsh realities of Asian power politics – with the growth of the Soviet Pacific fleet, the Indonesian annexation of East Timor and the Vietnamese occupation of Kampuchea. They fear criticism of their immigration policy lest it should appear anti-Asian and any pressures for mass immigration which would threaten their European lifestyle. Their exports of food and raw materials draw them towards the expanding economies of Japan, South-East Asia and China. Conversely, the need to preserve Australian industry behind high tariff barriers clouds relations with Asia and Australian labour relations are harshly criticised by the more efficient Asian nations. All this is part of the process of adjustment as Australia becomes increasingly a nation in its own right – instead of an appendage of Europe or the US – and as the Asian nations develop. The opportunities far outweigh the threats but fears acquired over generations cannot be shaken off in a decade. The threat from China is no longer a preoccupation but Asia is still viewed with a strong measure of apprehension.

8 Indochina: An Arena of Conflict

SIR JOHN ADDIS

My subject is Indochina – an arena of conflict. It is a large subject and in an attempt to make it more manageable, I am going to consider conflict in the sense of competing national interests. Over the past thirty years or so, the interests of France, the United States, China and the Soviet Union have met and conflicted with each other in the peninsula of Indochina, and all have conflicted with the aspirations of the Vietnamese Communists.

Those aspirations have been clear and consistent: independence, socialism – in the Marxist–Leninist sense – and reunification, since unity became an issue in 1954. In pursuing these aims, the Vietnamese of Ho Chi Minh's party have been uncompromising. In their resistance to the French they never adopted a united front policy, as the Chinese Communists did. The Vietnamese have always rejected compromise and have favoured confrontation. Theirs was an all or nothing strategy. And they have also pursued their aim with an unremitting sense of urgency. Here again there is a difference from the Chinese Communists who have always taken the long view, and been prepared not only to compromise and reach tactical accommodation with their adversaries, but also to wait for the propitious concatenation of circumstances when they might advance a step further towards their long-term goal.

Not so the Vietnamese. For them not only is compromise unacceptable, but so also is delay: they have felt compelled always to press on relentlessly to achieve their total desiderata in the shortest possible time. I do not mean that the Chinese Communists have been any less devoted to ultimate total victory in the attainment of their objectives than the Vietnamese, or even that all the basic objectives of the Chinese and Vietnamese have been incompatible. The difference between the two is one of timing and tactics. The Chinese are prepared to compromise and wait; the Vietnamese never.

There is no need to spend time on Vietnamese resistance to the attempt to reimpose French authority from 1945 to 1954. The resistance was led by Ho Chi Minh and the Vietnam Workers Party, a Communist Party established on Stalinist lines. Independence was the primary aim, and for Ho Chi Minh and his party, socialism, in the Marxist–Leninist sense, was a *sine qua non* of independence. The two aims, independence and socialism, were inseparable.

The conflict between the Vietnamese and the French led directly to American involvement in Indochina. American influence in Asia generally had been greatly expanded by the victory over the Japanese. US forces were established in Japan and South Korea. The United States was also heavily engaged in China. The attempt to reconcile the Nationalists and the communists in China failed. And when the civil war broke out again in 1947, the United States pursued a forward policy by giving active support to the Nationalists. That policy failed too.

AMERICAN POLICY

At this distance of time, it is possible to view the United States appreciation of the world situation in 1950 dispassionately. The establishment of the People's Republic of China in 1949 was a defeat for American policies four years after the great victory over Japan. Communism was widely held to be monolithic – an extension of communism in the Soviet Union. China was even sometimes seen to be little more than the tool or agent of the Soviet Union. The victory over Germany had been immediately followed by the forcible spread of communism to the countries of Eastern Europe. It was widely assumed in the West that communism by its nature was necessarily expansive in this way. The expectation therefore was that communism in China would inevitably spill over the frontiers of China to take over neighbouring countries.

A prime concern of American policy in Asia therefore was to

stem the expansion of the communist flood tide. The two assumptions on which this basic policy was founded were both mistaken. The People's Republic of China and the Soviet Union were even then not monolithically united; and China in 1950 had far too many domestic problems to seek foreign adventures. But the belief in the inevitability of Chinese Communist expansion was devoutly held, so devoutly that resistance to it was inspired by an almost crusading spirit.

American resistance to communism in China was not merely reactive and defensive. It was prepared to take the initiative in advancing what, in the jargon of the time, were called the frontiers of the free world. This meant that American policy at the time was expansionist in the sense of being concerned to expand American influence to areas where that influence had not been dominant before.

The United States had no love for the restoration of European colonialism in Asia. But the opponents of French colonialism in Indochina were communists. And from May 1950 the United States decided to give France military supplies for the war in Indochina. This military aid to France for Indochina was given one month before the outbreak of the Korean war. An American Military Assistance Advisory Group was set up in Indochina in August 1950, three months before the entry of Chinese troops into Korea. From early 1952 the Pentagon was considering contingency plans for action against China if China intervened in Indochina. In April 1954 a Joint Staff Agency met in Pearl Harbor for this purpose – the United States, the United Kingdom, France, Australia and New Zealand. This meeting took place before the fall of Dienbienphu.

American reluctance to go along with the Geneva settlement on Indochina is well-documented and well-known, and in the years that followed they frustrated its implementation in South Vietnam in 1956, with the refusal to hold elections, and in Laos in 1958, with the installation of the Phoui Sananikone government.

The Korean armistice of 1953 on the other hand provided a solution that has endured because the south was solidly anti–communist. South Vietnam at the time of the Geneva conference was already so riddled with insurgency that it could not be made into a secure bastion. The American attempts to support the regime in the south were bound from the start to fail. American policy in Laos up to 1960 was also incapable of success. Laos was so intrinsically weak that it could never have been made into an effective shield or bastion. Laos would have served American interests better as a weak and neutral buffer. But American policy disapproved of neutrality and preferred direct confrontation across a clearly defined line. Sihanouk's equivocal neutrality irked them, but for the time being they could not alter it.

From 1964 US Air Forces and from 1965 US ground forces were committed to shoring up the regime in South Vietnam. It can be seen now that the objective was never capable of attainment. The process of disengagement began from 1968, and the American military commitment in Vietnam was brought to an end in January 1973.

CHINA AND VIETNAM

The Chinese were also engaged in the conflicts in Indochina after 1945. Vietnamese memories of centuries of resistance to Chinese domination are still lively. But Vietnam also belongs to the Chinese cultural world, and state and society in Vietnam share the Confucian tradition. There were affinities as well as divisive issues inherited from the past. In the present, the ruling parties in both countries are cast in the mould of Leninism and Stalinism.

From 1948 there was contact on the frontier between communist-led forces in China and in Vietnam. From 1950 there was agreement to clear up the frontier area so that Chinese supplies could reach the Vietminh. A very senior representative of the Chinese Central Committee was sent to Vietnam, and a Military Advisory Group was set up there under Wei Guoqing, who became the head of the General Political Department of the People's Liberation Army. It looks as if from 1950 until the Geneva Conference in 1954 there was smooth fraternal cooperation between the Vietminh and the Chinese in the pursuit of a shared objective.

China's aims at the Geneva Conference on Indochina come out clearly. The overriding objective was to prevent the development of another war like Korea on China's southern flank. Korea had been a terrible experience for China. The worst eventuality, the spread of the fighting to China itself and the bombing of the industrial base in the north-east, had been avoided. But China had paid a terrible price – the loss of between half and one million killed, the frustration of the operation to take Taiwan, the failure to reunify China and end the civil war, exclusion from the United Nations, the embargo, and diversion of scarce resources from the tasks of socialist revolution and construction. The lesson of the Korean experience for China in the context of Indochina was that the Americans must not become so involved there that the Chinese would have to intervene to confront them militarily. The nightmare for China was a repetition of Korea in Indochina. In April 1954, before the Geneva Conference opened, the Chinese told the Vietnamese: 'China cannot openly assist Vietnam in the event of expansion of the conflict there'. The import of that communication is clear. If America intervened in Indochina the Chinese would not come in openly against them as they had done in Korea.

The Korean solution had been a ceasefire without a political settlement. The three years of fighting were brought to an end with a simple return to the *status quo ante* division along a parallel of latitude. The Korean solution provided for the Chinese the model of what should be sought at Geneva for Indochina – armistice without a political settlement, and division along a parallel of latitude even though that involved the partition of Vietnam.

This was the solution which was in fact accepted, willingly or reluctantly, by all the parties to the conference. It was very different from what the Vietminh wanted. As always, their own choice was to go flat out for the final victory. They claim now that after Dienbienphu they could have defeated the French completely. That is a plausible claim. But even if these high hopes had not been immediately justified, they would surely have preferred to go on fighting, rejecting all compromise and the constraint of an armistice. It was clear enough at the time that the solution of an armistice at Geneva was imposed on a very unwilling Vietnamese delegation by strong pressure from both the Russians and the Chinese. The Vietnamese now speak of Chinese betrayal at Geneva, without mentioning the part played by the Russians.

The Chinese were, however, well enough content with the Geneva agreement and, indeed, made great efforts and considerable concessions to make it possible. American intervention, which had been directly threatened during the Dienbienphu campaign immediately before the conference, had been avoided. The Americans were now kept at bay south of the 17th Parallel. Between their presence and the Chinese frontier there was the comforting barrier of a Communist, and therefore anti-American, state. At the request of Ho Chi Minh, China sent a team of experts headed by Fang Yi to help with the rehabilitation of North Vietnam. But they also made an offer to establish relations with Saigon, which was not accepted by Diem.

The Vietnamese consulted China and the Soviet Union about what their policy should be in the aftermath of the Geneva conference. The Chinese advice was that the procedure of elections prescribed at Geneva could not lead to reunification because of United States opposition. They advised the Vietnamese to prepare for a protracted struggle. Deng Xiaoping told them a year later in July 1955 that the attempt to reunify by force entailed unacceptable risks to the security of North Vietnam. Mao in November 1956 told them that reunification was not possible in a short time: 'If 10 years is not enough, we should be prepared for 100 years'. In July 1957 Mao told them that the important thing was to defend the 17th Parallel and again spoke of a solution taking a long time. In 1958 the Vietminh proposed to the Chinese that armed struggle should be adopted as the policy for South Vietnam. The Chinese advised them not to expose their armed forces in South Vietnam and said they thought the time was not yet ripe.

The Chinese advice for caution and the long view must have been most unwelcome and irksome to the Vietminh. In late 1959 there were uprisings in the south, and this seemed to settle the debate whether the right policy was political struggle or armed struggle. Hanoi promptly decided to turn to a policy of combining political and armed struggle in the south. The Chinese did not approve. On 14th May 1960 Zhou Enlai on a visit to Hanoi told the Vietnamese that neither political struggle nor armed struggle would result in an immediate seizure of power in the south. Even the collapse of the Diem regime, he said, would not bring about immediate reunification, because the Americans would never allow it. He advised Hanoi to give only political support to the south, and to refrain from military support until they were sure of success, that is 'when it is quite certain that nothing bad can happen.' He again said that the struggle remained a long one. However, before the end of the year, the Chinese had changed their minds. They told the Vietnamese that they now agreed on a policy of armed struggle in the south and would support it. In December 1960, they were the first to recognise the National Liberation Front of South Vietnam.

In the summer of 1962 Ho Chi Minh went himself to China to ask for military support for the armed forces in South Vietnam. China agreed to send 90,000 'armed weapons', which does not seem very generous. More important, from about this time they opened a supply route to South Vietnam from Hanoi through Sihanoukville. In 1963 the Chinese tried to enlist Vietnamese support in their struggle with the Soviet Union for the allegiance of world communist parties but were rebuffed. That created another cause of antagonism between the two parties.

Direct American involvement in the fighting in Vietnam, from February 1965, introduced a new stage. The Chinese still advised the Vietnamese that the right policy was protracted war, guerrilla warfare, small battles. In March and April the Chinese rejected Soviet proposals, which the Vietnamese had welcomed, for joint action which would have involved the use of Chinese territory by Soviet aircraft in support of Vietnam. Early in April 1965 Le Duan went to Beijing to ask for Chinese volunteers for Vietnam, no doubt on the Korean precedent. It seems from rather divergent accounts that the Chinese agreed to send anti-aircraft teams and army engineers but not pilots or infantry. The Chinese units started to arrive in October 1965 and reached a peak of 170,000 at one time. In 1966 the Chinese rejected Vietnamese proposals for a united international front in support of Vietnam because they would not agree that the front should include the Soviet Union. In autumn 1966 the Vietnamese suggested to the Chinese that the policy should be fighting combined with negotiations, that is to say, another form of combining political and military warfare. Zhou Enlai advised them that in China's experience victory at the conference table was only to be obtained when it had been won on the battlefield.

The Tet offensive in early 1968 ran exactly counter to the Chinese advice of protracted war, guerrilla warfare, small battles. Though, militarily, it failed to take Saigon, it had an important and perhaps decisive effect on morale in the United States. At the end of March President Johnson made an offer to negotiate.

Hanoi accepted promptly, without first notifying Beijing or even consulting Ho, who was in Beijing for medical treatment. The Chinese therefore maintained a conspicuous reserve throughout the United States–Vietnamese talks from May to October 1968. In April 1968 they told the Vietnamese that they had not yet secured a favourable position for negotiating with the Americans, and that they had been making concessions too hastily. Chinese reservations about Vietnamese negotiations with the Americans appear to have been maintained consistently until 1971.

By July 1970 all the Chinese military personnel had been withdrawn from Vietnam. Yet Chinese aid to Vietnam was increased in 1971–72. Frankly I do not know how to interpret those two developments.

A new phase was introduced with Dr Henry Kissinger's first visit to Beijing in July 1971. In the broadest terms, Kissinger was negotiating a new geopolitical relationship between the United States and the People's Republic of China. In narrower terms, he was bargaining for Chinese help in securing an armistice in Indochina in return for American withdrawal from Taiwan. It was on this dual basis that agreement was concluded in February 1972 at the end of President Nixon's visit. On Kissinger's evidence, China in November 1971 urged Vietnam to accept the American terms for a ceasefire, and again a year later. On 5th December 1972, the Chinese acted as Nixon's mouthpiece to convey a threat of the consequences of holding out against an agreement, and this threat was carried out by the B-52s. China's attitude to negotiations between Vietnam and the United States had therefore been reversed. There was no longer the insistence that a solution at the conference table must await a favourable situation on the battlefield. Having agreed with Kissinger that progress on Indochina should take precedence over progress on Taiwan, the Chinese were now urging the Vietnamese to speed up with the negotiations for a ceasefire.

Vietnam's position in Laos and Cambodia was also a cause of tension between Vietnam and China. I think the case is proven that Hanoi has always wanted a dominant position in Laos and Cambodia and has never given up that ambition. It is one of the quirks of history in this century that former colonies on attaining independence accept as sacrosanct the boundaries which had been quite arbitrarily imposed by colonialism. Laos and Cambodia lie outside the Confucian culture of Vietnam, and Laos in particular has much closer affinities with Thailand than with Vietnam.

It is abundantly clear that today China is firmly opposed to the exercise of control over Laos and Cambodia by Vietnam, now an ally of China's chief enemy, the Soviet Union. But if there had not been the Soviet factor, would China have opposed Vietnamese dominance in Indochina? It is difficult to be sure. There are only scraps of evidence.

Hanoi probably enjoyed effective control of the Laotian Party from as early as the 1950s. Perhaps for this reason, China for some years was curiously inactive in Laos. The Chinese appear to have made no attempt to influence internal developments in Laos in the 1950s and early 1960s. They did not even establish diplomatic relations until September 1962. The road-building programme in northern Laos dates from 1964, and even then does not seem to have been exploited politically by the Chinese. After the end of the fighting in 1975, Laos was in effect taken over by Vietnam before the end of the year without China lifting a finger.

In Cambodia, China appears to have been more active in asserting its influence against the Vietnamese. Pol Pot went to Beijing in 1965 and from that year China was in touch with his guerrillas in Cambodia. In October 1972 and January 1973 Le Duan told Kissinger that while the Vietnamese could speak for the resistance in Laos, they could not guarantee results in bringing the fighting in Cambodia to a stop. The Vietnamese now allege that in the second half of 1975 a large number of Chinese advisers were with Pol Pot while he carried out the evacuation of the cities and his other extreme measures. If that charge is well-founded, the Chinese advisers must surely have been under the influence of the Gang of Four in Beijing. Some of Pol Pot's measures, such as the abolition of currency and commodity exchange, were the practical application of ideas ventilated in articles by doctrinaire extremists in Beijing such as Zhang Chongquiao in 1958, during the Cultural Revolution and again in 1975.

The conflict between China and Vietnam came into the open in the summer of 1978 in a dispute over their common border and the question of the ethnic Chinese in Vietnam. But those were probably secondary issues. The prime cause of the quarrel was surely what Kissinger would call geopolitical, that is to say, the influence exercised in the peninsula by Vietnam perceived as an ally of the Soviet Union.

The Chinese incursion into Vietnam in February/March 1979 was for the professed purpose of teaching Vietnam a lesson. The operation took longer than planned and resulted in heavy Chinese losses of men and material. Installations in the occupied area were ruthlessly destroyed, and this probably achieved the objective of delaying Vietnam's economic rehabilitation, and so of reducing her ability to maintain secure control of Cambodia and Laos.

China's policy now is to exercise multiple pressures to prevent Vietnam consolidating effective control over Laos and Cambodia and restoring its own strength after the ravages of prolonged war. Those pressures include the sustained threat of a second military incursion, economic sanctions and the mobilisation of the forces opposing the recognition of Heng Samrin's Government. They seem to have some hopes that those pressures if sustained may bring some results within not more than a few years.

VIETNAM AND THE SOVIET UNION

In the current polemic with China much has been revealed of relations between China and Vietnam since Geneva and almost nothing of relations with the Soviet Union. Yet it is certain that at Geneva the Soviet Union as well as China pressed the reluctant Vietnamese to agree to a settlement. Hoang Van Hoan, the dissident Vietnamese who has gone over to Beijing, has revealed that after Geneva the Soviet Union advised Hanoi to pursue a policy of peaceful coexistence and to achieve reunification by peaceful measures on the basis of independence and democracy. It is surely a fair assumption that at all times and especially since 1956 the Soviet Union, no less than China, has pursued its own national interests in regard to Indochina, and that those interests have not uniformly coincided with the aspirations of Hanoi. The Soviet Union's national interest in Indochina is clearly to extend her worldwide domination, particularly the security of sea routes, and to complete the encirclement of China. If and when a breach comes between Vietnam and the Soviet Union, there will no doubt be revelations of many strains and frictions in that relationship which are not yet apparent.

9 Korea's Changing Security Environment

RICHARD SIM

Discussion of Korean security tends towards oversimplification; to an analysis of the size and imminence of a communist assault upon the South. Yet in the mid- to late 1980s this issue itself is contingent upon several factors: the attitudes of the great powers, the possible acquisition of nuclear weapons by the two Koreas, the development of intra-Korean relations, the succession in the North, and most critically of all, the continuing dynamic growth of the South Korean economy.

Korea's geostrategic position – contiguous to the two main communist powers and athwart vital sea lanes to Japan – makes it intrinsically important to the United States, Japan, the Soviet Union and China. South Korea's burgeoning economic strength is a considerable prize in its own right while, of course, the continuing safeguarding of Seoul's putative democracy makes the future of Korea something of a test of American commitment to the defence of non-Communist Asia. Since the end of the Korean War (1950–53), the peninsula has enjoyed three decades of peace but it has been a peace fraught with danger, for since the failure of the Geneva Peace Conference on Korea in 1954 there have been no concerted efforts to reach a comprehensive peace agreement. On the contrary, both states remain locked in confrontation, heavily armed and primed for instant action, though they have been engaged in a measure of dialogue since 1984.

Given the history of government in Korea it is perhaps not too surprising that authoritarian regimes prevail both in North and South Korea. Until quite recent years the Koreans had never known a democratic system. Since the fourteenth century there has been a strong tradition of centralised government extending down to the village level. The conformist tradition of Confucianism has also left its mark on the Korean political mind. Since the Korean War successive South Korean governments have invoked the need for security against attack or subversion by North Korea as justification for restrictive policies towards political liberty. These and other factors have sometimes led Western observers to question Seoul's democratic credentials. Yet while it is true that the realities of South Korea's position have given it a political character considerably different from that of the Western democracies, it still enjoys a recognisably representative system and an incomparably freer one than that found in the North. Continuing provocative behaviour by the North coupled with memories of the communist onslaught which started the Korean War naturally tend therefore to locate the source of tension in the Korean peninsula firmly with the Pyongyang leadership.

THE PROBLEMS OF NORTH KOREA

North Korea's reputation in the West is justifiably suspect. The North's cult of Kim Il Sung provokes an automatic repugnance among most Westerners, while the drug trafficking of its diplomats, its sponsorship of terrorism abroad and its seemingly endless military build-up only serve to confirm the impression of an unsavoury depotism geared up for aggression and mayhem. Understandably, it has become something of a pariah in the international community.

The grounds for continuing apprehension are real. Pyongyang has maintained a fierce and unstinting propaganda war against the South and its American benefactor for many years. This has been supplemented by a number of outrages, most notably the October 1983 Rangoon bombing which murdered four South Korean ministers; constant tunnelling under the Demilitarised Zone (DMZ), the seizure of the Pueblo, the murder of US officers in the DMZ, and the attempted shooting down of US Blackbird reconnaissance aircraft. The Rangoon incident alone in an earlier time might well have been regarded as an act of war. Other indicators of Pyongyang's aggressive intentions are not hard to find. The North continually claims to be the only sovereign

Korean government; it is unstinting in its efforts to have Seoul ostracised in the international arena; maintains an impressive rate of military expansion; and concentrates its forces overwhelmingly near the DMZ. Moreover, according to American estimates, North Korea has some 835,000 men under arms compared with 622,000 South Koreans and 39,000 Americans. All this is particularly unsettling to Seoul, the political and economic nerve centre of the South. A mere 25 miles from the DMZ, Seoul was captured by North Korean troops within three days of their surprise attack in 1950 and is now only a heart beat away from the North Korean air force. Intelligence gleaned from defectors tends to confirm the view that the present deployment and training of North Korean forces is still orientated towards an imminent attack upon the South.

Certainly also the aura of mystery which surrounds the reclusive leadership in Pyongyang would be of great assistance in mounting a surprise attack. In recent years the North is known to have enacted a number of measures designed to exploit the advantages of a surprise attack. Most notably it has established the world's largest commando force numbering some 100,000 soldiers. They have been trained and equipped to move rapidly through Korea's mountainous terrain immediately after the first onslaught and then to operate as substantial disruptive guerrilla units behind the front line. The mobile capacity of the North Korean army has been enhanced enormously by recent developments: by 1983 it had some 3,100 tanks, an increase of fully 2,300 over the 1973 figure; 1,500 armoured personnel carriers compared with 200 a decade earlier; and 1,500 self-propelled artillery pieces compared with zero in 1973. New equipment for the navy and air force, including 250 AN2 Soviet-made aircraft and some 100 high-speed landing craft should further assist a rapid assault strategy.

Yet it remains notoriously difficult to assess the actual intentions of this hermitic country. A pattern of provocation and arms build-up do not in themselves constitute a war policy, although they remain serious grounds for concern. In fact there is a growing amount of evidence to suggest that the 1980s will be a most unfavourable time for a possible North Korean attack, whatever the wishes of its leadership. In particular the growing economic imbalance between the two Koreas is likely to have serious repercussions on the strategic balance of the peninsula.

Because of this, domestic and particularly economic concerns are likely to be the North Korean priorities from 1984 onwards.

Internally the regime north of the 38th parallel appears to be well-established and to enjoy a measure of popular support. Certainly, the North's agriculture has been a significant success story in recent years; and the populace seems essentially well-provided for in terms of food, clothing and essential goods although, in common with most communist countries, lacking in consumer goods. There are however no reliable barometers of public opinion in such a tightly regimented society; and outside observers are excessively dependent on travellers' tales: it is possible that the rumours of mutinies in the North Korean army in 1982 point to a deeper malaise.

The regime's immediate preoccupations however seem clear: to sustain the cult of Kim Il Sung at home and to promote his son, Kim Jong Il, as successor. The key to legitimate succession in such a personalised dictatorship, where Kim Il Sung has been the effective ruler since the inception of the state, is to stress the continuity of the regime. Ostensibly this is being done. The sixth congress of the ruling Korean Workers' Party (KWP), held in 1980, endorsed Kim Jong Il as the presumed successor. He is now a member of the politburo of the KWP central committee, of the secretariat, and of the party's military commission. His succession therefore seems assured but there are repeated rumours of opposition to the move. The recent replacement of senior North Korean generals by younger officers may well be the consequence of a policy of deliberately phasing out opposition elements. Kim Jong Il's immediate entourage of party cadres are all of his generation. Thus two generations have been missed out in the promotion stakes, a fact which may stimulate factionalism within the ruling KWP. In that eventuality it is possible that bureaucratic purges may not be sufficient to remove opposition should a serious crisis follow Kim Il Sung's demise.

ECONOMIC DEVELOPMENTS

Whichever way the succession issue is eventually resolved, North Korean urgently needs to find a solution to the problem of its ailing economy, now trailing ominously behind the South. The Northern economy has been slowing since the early 1980s; and manufacturing industry is now generally held to be in great need of improving its plant and equipment. Unless the North invests more in its economy and secures access to advanced technical knowledge it will fall well behind the South. Time is now decisively on the side of the South as its economic strength is increasingly reflected militarily. North Korea currently enjoys a military advantage over the South but its equipment is ageing. The widening technological gap can only be bridged by a vast and as yet unanticipated improvement in the North's economic prospects. Yet on the contrary the North's sluggish growth rate makes it most improbable that it will retain its military advantages into the late 1980s. By 1983 South Korea's GNP was fully four times that of the North; all the expectations were that the difference would become greater. Yet it is hard to see how North Korea, shor' of massive aid from the Soviet Union, can hope to catch up with the South without becoming a more active member of the international community. This too will not easily be attained. North Korea enjoys an unenviably low credit rating and is well behind on the payment of interest on existing foreign loans.

North Korea does however seem to have some sense of a need to change its approach to foreign commerce. The traditional self-reliance or *chuche* policies seem increasingly inadequate. Indeed in January 1984 the Supreme People's Assembly stated its wish to do more trade with the West and Japan; but clearly a substantial period of preparation and negotiation will be necessary before any significant progress can be made in this direction. Yet such a radical departure could accord well with a change in the leadership in Pyongyang. Although the present emphasis is certainly on continuity it is a commonly observed fact of history that after the deaths of dictators their successors sometimes try to give a distinctive colouring to their own rule. A change of direction commercially would certainly be in line with North Korea's changing needs.

THE PROBLEMS OF REUNIFICATION

Thus changes in the economic balance between the two Koreas are making a militarily enforced unification increasingly more difficult to achieve than in 1950 while the relative economic decline of the North makes a peaceful *modus vivendi* with the South more desirable at least until some kind of rough equality can be restored. Yet even if the international climate in the mid-1980s may be becoming more favourable towards a constructive relationship than it has been since the end of the Korean War, there is still a lack of substantial effort towards easing tension. In the past mutual suspicion has meant that all prospects for a real dialogue between North and South have been strangled at an early stage. Both Seoul and Pyongyang primarily want to strengthen their position *vis-à-vis* the other. Although they speak of reunification as the ultimate goal both are really concerned to win advantage over the other. Most proposals for reunification are therefore made with the intention of putting the other side at a disadvantage by compelling an immediate rejection.

It was therefore doubly striking when on 8 October 1983, North Korea, possibly mindful of the country's changing strategic balance, proposed a new peace plan much more serious in content than any of the North's predecessors. Pyongyang's plan envisaged a two-tier resolution of the Korean problem: a negotiated settlement between the United States and the two Koreas leading to a peace settlement and a withdrawal of US troops from the peninsula; and bilateral talks between Pyongyang and Seoul aimed at bringing about national reunification.

The novel feature of the plan was that the North Koreans have never before countenanced making Seoul a party to any peace talks, a *de facto* partial recognition which gave the plan a plausibility it would otherwise have lacked. This was a significant change in both tone and substance.

South Korea was quick to reject the tripartite proposals, a position endorsed by President Reagan who suggested that four-way talks would be better. This would have been a much more satisfactory face-saving idea for Seoul also, which in three-way talks would almost certainly be placed in an inferior position. The inclusion of China, ally and benefactor of the North, would however resolve this problem. Aside from any merit in the proposals their rejection was perhaps inevitable in view of their extraordinary timing, only 24 hours before the Rangoon bomb blast. Indeed in rejecting the North's proposals the South Korean Minister of Unification, Sohn Jae Shik, said that peace negotiations could not begin until Pyongyang admitted responsibility and apologised for the Rangoon bombing of

9 October 1983 which killed 21 people, including four South Korean ministers. Nonetheless, despite this major extenuating circumstance, the negative attitude of Seoul and Washington was undoubtedly embarrassing as former Presidents Carter and Park Chung Hee had proposed exactly such a tripartite conference in the summer of 1979. On that occasion it was the North which rejected it.

It seems then that a peace settlement can only begin to be discussed if China, and possibly the Soviet Union as well, is included in discussions. Moscow and Beijing continue to give support for North Korea and particularly to the North's demand for the withdrawal of US military forces. Yet it is most unlikely that either would like to see Pyongyang again attempt to upset the *status quo* by military action. Much has been made of China's alleged influence in Pyongyang and it is true that China's present attitude is one of extreme caution. Beijing certainly does not want another war in Korea but equally it is most unlikely to exert itself to persuade Pyongyang to seek a comprehensive peace treaty. Because Kim Il Sung has skilfully maintained cordial relations with Moscow, the Chinese are anxious not to pressurise the North Koreans into turning to the Russians.

The Soviet Union itself is a much less visible actor in Korean affairs than China but its interest in the security of North-East Asia is substantial. The dangers of Soviet involvement in a future Korean conflict are potentially enormous. The Soviet Union is an ominously powerful neighbour and has long been projecting considerable naval forces into the Pacific and deploying an increasing number of SS-20 missiles and Backfire bombers in the East. Certainly Russian involvement in a future conflict in the region would at the very least jeopardise the American ability to reinforce her 38,000 ground troops in Korea. Nor is the Soviet military entirely absent from the Korean military scene itself. There is constant Soviet surveillance of American exercises in the area. Indeed, on 21 March 1984 the US aircraft carrier Kitty Hawk collided with a nuclear-powered Soviet submarine in the Sea of Japan. It took place only about 150 miles from the South Korean coastline during the Team Spirit '84 exercises. Pyongyang itself, although apparently tilting more to Beijing, must look to Moscow for any future imports of sophisticated weaponry. The North's debts to the USSR are already colossal. Moreover, in 1982 the Soviet Union went to some lengths to emphasise the dependence of North Korean industry on Soviet assistance, a claim which incidentally automatically undermined Pyongyang's much trumpeted claims to self-sufficiency.

South Korea itself was keenly aware of the need to achieve some kind of *rapprochement* with the two major communist powers if a lasting solution to the Korean problem was to be found. Only the Soviet Union's unprovoked shooting down of a South Korean airliner in 1983 broke off Seoul's tentative approaches. Not long before the downing of the KAL airliner South Korea's then foreign minister, Lee Bum Suk, speaking at the National War College had called for a big effort to improve South Korea's relations with the socialist world, including China and the Soviet Union. He deliberately termed his policy *Nordpolitik* consciously evoking memories of Western Germany's *Ostpolitik* which had led to a thaw in Bonn's relations with Eastern Europe. Prior to this Seoul had already launched a number of bridge-building operations designed to court Moscow and Beijing but these presumably were now to be accelerated. One test was to be the holding in October 1983 in the South Korean capital of the 70th conference of the Inter-Parliamentary Union (IPU). Not only the Soviet Union but also Cuba, Hungary, Poland and Czechoslovakia were confidently expected to send delegations. However the KAL atrocity abruptly scuttled such initiatives and probably set back Seoul's hopes of improving relations with Moscow for years to come. Doubtless Pyongyang which publicly supported the Soviet action was the only government genuinely pleased by the event.

The USSR despite its potential considerable leverage on the North Korean regime is unlikely in any case to encourage a settlement. After Chernenko took power in February 1984 it appeared that the Soviet Union was even less concerned about its image abroad and quite prepared to see relations with the West deteriorate further. Far from seeking accommodation with the West it seemed that the Kremlin was in favour of taking a more assertive role to counter President Reagan's vigorous global foreign policy. Indications of this were the use of unprecedented high altitude bombing in Afghanistan, the boycott of the Olympic Games and the harsher treatment of the Sakharovs. Moscow indeed might even be tempted to step up its involvement in the Middle East or Central America in order to cause the United States more difficulties. Although a deliberate policy of stepping-up pressure on the Korean issue seemed most unlikely, an increasingly hawkish policy would certainly not help towards a relaxation of tensions in Korea.

THE OUTLOOK

In the final analysis President Reagan's insistence on wider involvement in Korean negotiations is probably right. Indeed it is hard to envisage a comprehensive settlement of the Korean problem which would not in the end necessitate the involvement of all interested parties, including Japan and the USSR. In the present climate of international relations such a settlement is impossible.

By the late 1980s the overall balance between the two Koreas will have changed. The dynamic growth of the South's economy is certain to be a critical factor. The logic of the South's sustained growth and its readiness to spend increasingly high sums on defence means quite simply that the North will not be able to keep pace. The roughly equal balance of military power in the peninsula in the early 1980s will towards the end of the decade have tilted in Seoul's favour.

There is however a small danger here that as the South becomes more independent and assumes more responsibility for its own defence, Seoul may be tempted to seek a nuclear arms capability. However, granted the firmness of the Reagan administration's commitment to the defence of the South, this must remain a remote contingency.

The North Koreans faced with a dynamic southern economy that they can not match may then feel obliged to appeal to Moscow and Beijing for much greater military assistance, thus triggering an accelerated arms race on the peninsula. However, Pyongyang is unlikely to launch an attack unless all US forces have been withdrawn and it is assured that China and/or the USSR will rush in military hardware immediately after the start of an attack; and that South Korea is showing signs of being internally ungovernable. A congruence of such factors in the late 1980s can be ruled out.

A more plausible basis for modest optimism may be that as North Korea's military edge begins to ebb it will increasingly feel bound to deal with the Western countries and Japan thereby

providing more scope for informal cross-recognition agreements
whereby the USSR and China have more contacts with South
Korea; and the US more with the North.

Part III
Regional Cooperation

10 The Role and Paradox of ASEAN

MICHAEL LEIFER

In discussing the Association of South-East Asian Nations, or ASEAN, which comprises Thailand, Malaysia, Singapore, Indonesia and the Philippines and, since January 1984, Brunei, it is important to adopt a realistic sense of perspective and to avoid employing false criteria.

First, ASEAN does not constitute an economic community along the lines of the model of Europe. Indeed, the very nature of ASEAN's economies militates against the prospect of a common market. Trade liberalisation has been a limited and protracted process. Economic cooperation has been most viable in the form of corporate bargaining with industrialised dialogue partners. Second, it is not a defence community like NATO. The problem of defence cooperation turns not only on appropriate aggregate capability but also on corresponding strategic perspectives. Defence cooperation requires a common sense of external threat which has never distinguished the regional partnership. I would suggest it is more suitable to regard ASEAN as a diplomatic community, if of a limited kind. Indeed, its limitations are in part a product of evident constraints on economic and military cooperation.

It should be emphasised also that ASEAN has always functioned on a strictly intergovernmental basis. As such it has been beset by a number of conflicts of interest which have been brought and contained within the walls of the Association. Indeed the ability to manage intra-mural tensions has become a distinctive feature of its activities underpinned by an established practice of bureaucratic and ministerial consultation.

That said, I wish to discuss ASEAN under three headings.

First, I intend to look at the nature of its evolution since its formation in August 1967. Second, I intend to consider the nature of its collective response to the third Indochina war which began with Vietnam's invasion of Cambodia (now Kampuchea) in December 1978. Third, I intend to look at the issue of military cooperation.

EVOLUTION

Before ASEAN was established the record of regional cooperation in South-East Asia had been chequered. Exercises in regional cooperation had been not only feeble but also divisive. One can point to false starts being made with the Association of South-East Asia (ASA), established in 1961, and also with a curious entity known by acronym as Maphilindo established for a while in 1963, and which was no more than a superficial device to try to resolve the controversy over the contentious advent to Malaysia. The public identities of these two bodies served to express adverse conceptions of what ought to be the appropriate basis for regional relationships. In the event, ASEAN when it was formed represented a merger of the membership of these two bodies with the exception of an independent Singapore.

The key to its advent was internal political change in Indonesia. An abortive *coup* in October 1965 had a catalytic effect; its failure and the reaction from the armed forces and the Moslems exposed the vulnerability of Indonesia's Communist Party and exposed also the political fragility of the position of President Sukarno. In other words, it served to undermine two of the three pillars upon which stood Indonesia's political system of Guided Democracy. That abortive *coup* and its consequences not only made possible an internal transfer of power in Indonesia to military advantage in March 1966, but also led to the revision of the political identity of the Indonesian state. That revision was expressed in part by the end of the confrontation against Malaysia in August 1966 and also in the new Indonesian Government's desire for regional reconciliation.

The extensive size, population, resources and the regional position of Indonesia made the disposition of its Government decisive for regional cooperation. If the other four member states had combined together it would have been significant, but without the membership of Indonesia that significance would have been much diminished. Thus when a romantic nationalism in Jakarta gave way to a conservative realism, it extended a pattern of conformity among five regional governments in terms of common attitudes to political order and economic development, and also in terms of their external affiliations. ASEAN represented the institutional expression of that extended pattern of conformity.

The instrumental priority of ASEAN was reconciliation because the disputes which beset its membership were not only between Malaysia and Indonesia but also extended beyond to the other three states. The prime object of the regional exercise was the promotion of a structure of relations which would serve to reinforce the domestic bases of conservative-minded governments by reducing external frictions between them.

The public priorities of ASEAN at its advent were economic growth, social progress and cultural development, which reflected internal needs of the respective states. Only secondary reference was made at the outset to problems of regional peace and stability. Apart from the realisation that recent adversaries would need time to develop the habit of cooperation, there was also a common concern to avoid being identified as a substitute for the American inspired South-East Asia Treaty Organisation (SEATO). Nonetheless, the advent of ASEAN was somewhat contentious and drew a hostile response from communist capitals.

The early experience of ASEAN was not promising. The scope of economic cooperation was limited; a factor which arose from the competitive relationship of the ASEAN economies, with the exception of Singapore, but even the island-state was viewed in a competitive light. It was evident that the viability of the Association could not rest on such feeble economic foundations. In addition, shortly after its formation there occurred a revival of 'intra-mural' conflict, that is, conflict between members of the Association. In 1968, there was a renewal in contentious circumstances of the Philippine claim to Sabah which led to an interruption in diplomatic relations between Malaysia and the Philippines. In 1968 also a stormy encounter occurred when the Singapore Government hanged two Indonesian marines who had been found guilty of sabotage and murder during the period of confrontation, and provoked a hostile response from Indonesia.

In the light of those episodes, it seemed evident that the promise of reconciliation was being dissipated.

If ASEAN was born out of conflict, then conflict served as a source of its revival, and that revival expressed itself above all in political cooperation. It indicated that the assumption that economic cooperation would serve the common cause of political stability had limited practical basis in the circumstances of the ASEAN states in the late 1960s. Yet if there was still an absence of any strong compulsion to openly assert a common political role, concurrent radical changes in the regional environment of the member states obliged the governments of ASEAN to re-examine the utility of political cooperation. One response to the change in the balance of external influences bearing on the region – arising in particular from American policy – took the form of greater bureaucratic and ministerial consultation.

The initial responses of the ASEAN states to changes in the balance of external influences bearing on South-East Asia were individual rather than collective. For example, an informal if premature attempt was made at an opening to China by the Foreign Minister of Thailand, Thanat Khoman, during 1969. Indonesia convened a conference on Cambodia in Jakarta in May 1970 which was less than successful as a diplomatic occasion and which demonstrated less than complete solidarity among the ASEAN states. Finally, Malaysia put forward a plan for the neutralisation of all of South-East Asia; a condition to be guaranteed by the major powers.

The reaction of other ASEAN states to that unilateral initiative indicated an absence of a common strategic perspective, and in the event, in November 1971, its Foreign Ministers acting outside the formal auspices of the Association reached a compromise on a common external policy aspiration which was in effect a dilution of the original Malaysian proposal. This alternative proposal, which was very hastily put together and could even have been drawn from a hat because there were a number of competing formulae, was a proposal for the establishment of a Zone of Peace, Freedom and Neutrality. If less than precise in prescription, it did represent a claim to design the fabric of regional order by excluding an intervening role for external powers, but in the absence of any corresponding capability to manage that order. Nonetheless, the direction in which the

ASEAN states were moving had been indicated, and in a sense the proposal did represent an element of continuity with part of the founding document of the Association. It also represented continuity in Indonesian strategic thinking which was not interrupted by the transfer of power from President Sukarno to Lieutenant-General Suharto in March 1966. However, the momentum in the evolution of ASEAN was not sustained. For example, subsequent *ad hoc* meetings of the Association on the recognition of the People's Republic of China and on developments in Indochina were not notable for expressing a sense of common purpose. Indeed, individual states went their own way on the question of recognition.

A critical formative event in the evolution of ASEAN was the success of revolutionary communism in Indochina during 1975. These dramatic events, particularly the successive falls of Phnom Penh and then Saigon, in April 1975, concentrated governmental minds. It reinforced a sense of shared predicament; it fore-shadowed regional polarisation and also competition on an ideological basis. There was an understood need to close ranks and to demonstrate solidarity. This was undertaken at the first ever meeting of heads of government of ASEAN held on the island of Bali in February 1976. In effect this event represented the political 'coming out' of ASEAN. Previously political priorities had been subordinated and dealt with informally. On Bali in an open statement of identity and purpose it was made clear that ASEAN was assuming a defined political role. For example, one of the two major documents arising from the conference was a Declaration of ASEAN Concord which openly articulated an agreement on the internal nature of primary threat, and identified the function of the Association, if not explicitly, as an internal collective security organisation. There was explicit agreement that internal security was indivisible among the partners of the Association. The heads of government also reaffirmed a commitment to the Zone of Peace proposal which had become the symbolic expression of a common external purpose. Secondly, a code of regional inter-state conduct was promulgated in a Treaty of Amity and Cooperation, with provision for accession by other South-East Asian States, which, in effect, constituted an opening to Indochina. A link was affirmed also between economic and political purpose which gave rise to meetings of

ASEAN Economic Ministers, and there was a measure of institutional development in confirming a prior decision to set up an ASEAN secretariat, if with only a service role.

One significant feature of Bali was that the summit meeting represented a measured and a fairly confident response to the fall of Indochina. It suggested an absence of any imminent sense of external threat. Bali was followed eighteen months later by a second meeting of heads of government, this time in Kuala Lumpur, to celebrate the tenth anniversary of the formation of ASEAN. The attendant process of evolution was somewhat fitful, however, with mixed fortunes experienced. For example, the ASEAN states were not able to develop a viable relationship with their counterparts in Indochina. Indeed, Vietnam and Laos had disputed the legitimacy of the Zone of Peace proposal at the conference of non-aligned countries which took place in Sri Lanka in August 1976, and also disputed by implication the right of the Association to prescribe for regional order in South-East Asia. In addition there was only modest progress in economic cooperation, especially over preferential trading arrangements.

On the other hand, there was some indication of an enhancement of ASEAN's collective role as a strengthened means of inter-state bargaining exemplified in the presence of the Japanese, Australian and New Zealand Prime Ministers at the Kuala Lumpur summit which established a precedent for subsequent ministerial meetings. Also from that time on, a regular process of dialogue was established between ASEAN as a corporate entity and a number of major states including Japan, the United States, as well as the European Community. Yet, if once again ASEAN was afflicted with a lack of momentum, once again regional conflict served as the source of the revival of its vitality.

The conflict between Vietnam and Kampuchea, which was publicly signalled at the end of 1977, stimulated competition for the political affections of the ASEAN states by contending communist governments and this competition served to enhance further the international standing of the Association. The need to respond in a coherent manner to a variety of external initiatives, including a diplomatic opening launched by the government in Hanoi, had the effect of improving the informal consultative machinery of the Association.

RESPONSE TO CONFLICT IN INDOCHINA

This brings me to the response of the Association to the conflict of Indochina. ASEAN evolved out of a sense of common predicament amongst its members, but without being able to forge a true unity of strategic purpose. Its measure of concordance had rested on the belief that political instability was indivisible among the five regional partners and, correspondingly, that political stability in one state would contribute to the attainment of that condition in all the others. The Indonesian government articulated this sense of linkage in its contribution of the terms national and regional resilience to the political vocabulary of ASEAN. However, a combination of varying domestic and communal circumstances and regional location served to deny the expression of a common strategic perspective. In other words, the five governments of ASEAN – in general accord over internal threat – have not been bound by a shared view of the principal source of external threat. This complex issue is best exemplified with reference to Indonesia and Thailand.

Indonesia, for its part as the largest and most important member state, has regarded China as its main long-term source of external threat but has viewed Vietnam as a natural counter to Chinese influence. On the other hand, Thailand, which certainly is not unconscious of China's threat potential, has been obliged to concentrate on the more immediate menace posed by Vietnam in Kampuchea, and has been willing to treat with China as a source of countervailing power.

Before Vietnam's invasion of Kampuchea, it was possible for ASEAN governments to accommodate alternative strategic perspectives without real difficulty. Indeed, one can suggest this was one of the symbolic functions of the Zone of Peace proposal to which all members could pay lip service and so demonstrate a sense of accord on external purpose. And as long as an independent and ferociously xenophobic Kampuchea denied the consolidation of Vietnamese dominance throughout Indochina, there was no requirement to think about a choice of strategic priorities, because there was no manifest external threat to any ASEAN state. Correspondingly, the attendant regional pattern of power was tolerable. Vietnam free of the undue influence of China satisfied Indonesian priorities, and an independent Kampuchea serving as an interposing buffer was acceptable to

Thailand and, as a matter of fact, also to Indonesia, which was on the point of setting up an embassy in Phnom Penh just prior to its investment by Vietnamese forces.

Vietnam's invasion of Kampuchea posed a dilemma for some ASEAN states, though less so for Thailand whose strategic environment had been violated. Indonesia with Malaysia, and to an extent the Philippines, which was the least affected by the assertion of Vietnamese power, had contemplated the utility of Vietnamese dominance in Indochina as a bulwark against an undue projection of Chinese influence southwards. These states, of course, were alarmed by Vietnam's violation of the cardinal rule of the society of states, particularly in the light of assurances of non-intervention which they had assumed had been given by Vietnam's Prime Minister Pham Van Dong during a tour of ASEAN capitals in September and October 1978. They were concerned also about the role of the Soviet Union in facilitating this violation. At the same time, they also had a view of Vietnam as a country pursuing an independent policy which was not tied to the interests of any external major power. Furthermore, they became apprehensive at the consequent act of punishment against Vietnam by China, and they held attendant concerns at the alternative prospects of either a politically debilitated Vietnam obliged to bend the knee to China, or a defiant Vietnam unduly dependent on the patrimony of the Soviet Union.

From Vietnam's invasion of Kampuchea, conflicting propensities have arisen within ASEAN which have turned on the issue of association with China and on the terms of a possible political settlement with Vietnam. During the continuing course of the Kampuchean conflict, the ASEAN states have, nonetheless, stood by their front-line partner, Thailand, and have sustained consistently a refusal to accord legitimacy to the government carried into Phnom Penh in the baggage train of the Vietnamese army. They have insisted also on the withdrawal of Vietnamese troops mobilising support within the United Nations to serve this end. They have also promoted a coalition of communist and non-communist Khmer resistance forces which was established at a meeting in Kuala Lumpur in June 1982.

Despite misgivings about Thailand's countervailing association with China, especially by Indonesia, and a fear that the

judgement of the Thai Government on which its policy is based –
namely, that Vietnam has over-reached itself – may be erroneous
and that therefore the confrontation over Kampuchea may be
self-defeating, ASEAN has sustained a remarkable solidarity
which has played a major role in denying international status to
Vietnam's client in Phnom Penh.

Why should this be so? First, there has been an absence of
any willingness on the part of Vietnam to compromise. It has
stuck to its maximal position that the situation in Kampuchea
is irreversible; it refuses to negotiate over returning Kampuchea
to the condition of a buffer state. That has been made explicit
by Vietnam's Foreign Minister Nguyen Co Thach on many
occasions. Given the persistent unwillingness to compromise on
the part of Vietnam, there does not seem to be much political
profit for any member state in breaking ASEAN ranks.

Second, there is a strong measure of awareness by ASEAN
governments of the stake which all members possess in the
continuing viability and coherence of the Association based on
their sense of common political identity and predicament, as
well as on the advantages of collective action. It is well understood
that any willingness to compromise with Vietnam, which is not
an expression of a corporate view, would prejudice the future of
the Association in its present form.

The commitment to ASEAN is expressed in diplomatic terms.
But the diplomatic strength of ASEAN alone cannot get to the
heart of the Kampuchean conflict. That strength has been
utilised to the advantage of the Association's front-line state,
Thailand, which does not rely on ASEAN as the prime means
to serve its own strategic interests. For Thailand, ASEAN serves
only as a supplementary tool in a strategy of military attrition
conducted primarily by the Khmer Rouge and by China supported
with economic sanctions by the United States and Japan which
is intended to weaken Vietnam over time until it releases hold
of Kampuchea. Accordingly, ASEAN has been caught up in a
process of conflict whose eventual resolution need not necessarily
reconcile the strategic interests of all of its member states. The
member states share a commitment to the Association which is
tied to a regional policy which is not supported wholeheartedly
by all regional partners. This paradox is part of the political
condition of ASEAN and a source of continuing inner tension.

MILITARY COOPERATION

This brings me to the issue of military cooperation. ASEAN is distinguished by another paradox. Its members have displayed a common interest in regional security. Yet the Association lacks the military capability and the quality of shared interests which are an essential precondition for alliance formation. This is not to say that ASEAN members do not engage in military cooperation. They do, in the form of exercises and maneouvres and the sharing of intelligence if primarily on a bilateral basis. Indeed, certain joint military operations, particularly across common borders, actually preceded the establishment of ASEAN. But this security cooperation has always been conducted outside the formal auspices of ASEAN. Even when ASEAN assumed explicitly a political identity at Bali, security cooperation was excluded from its formal purview. The Declaration of ASEAN Concord made provision for continuing cooperation on a non-ASEAN basis between member states in security matters in accordance with their needs and interests on this basis. When, in September 1982, Singapore's Prime Minister, Lee Kuan-yew advocated multilateral military exercises, he failed to attract any positive response from his regional partners.

There has been a consistent reluctance to transform the Association into an alliance. The conviction that the principal common threat is internal is still upheld; the corresponding view that alliance formation as opposed to informal *ad hoc* cooperation is not appropriate also prevails. Indeed, even the external military threat to Thailand, which some have seen as likely to bring about a change in ASEAN's attitude on this issue in the foreseeable future, is not a major stimulus because that threat has not been posed up to now against the country's territorial or political identity, but is directed against cross-border support for the Khmer Rouge resistance. Indeed, the Thai Government is reluctant to accept foreign troop deployments on its soil. It would prefer to demonstrate its unaided capability to defend territorial integrity. In circumstances of *extremis* it would be more likely to turn to a more substantial source of military capability, possibly the air power of the United States deployed from carriers offshore.

There is also an evident limitation to the aggregate military capability of ASEAN states despite increased spending on defence from the late 1970s. Most members have very little to spare from internal security roles, and apart from basic problems of logistics, there would be immense difficulty in concerting and coordinating ground troop deployments involving forces of different cultures and languages. Such a combined exercise would demand a level of sophisticated staff work which is beyond the present experience of the ASEAN military establishments. In addition of course there are still underlying mutual suspicions among ASEAN partners which gravitate against a ready willingness to accept foreign forces from one ASEAN state on the soil of another. It should be reiterated that alliances normally arise in response to a common view of external threat. ASEAN remains beset by an absence of a unified strategic perspective.

In addition, there has always been a concern among the ASEAN states lest formal military cooperation give rise to a sense of provocation and alarm especially in Hanoi. There has been concern also lest this occur without the prior establishment of a credible countervailing concert of power. Such recourse has not been viewed as the best way to induce Vietnam to join ultimately in a cooperative structure of regional relations.

The Vietnamese invasion of Kampuchea has of course affected the attitude of ASEAN governments towards external defence. In addition, the role of the Soviet Union in sustaining Vietnam with military assistance and logistical support and enjoying in return access to military facilities in Da Nang and Cam Ranh Bay has been observed with growing anxiety.

Nonetheless, there has not been any discernible change from the position articulated by President Suharto at Bali when he maintained concerning security cooperation, 'We have neither the capability nor the intention to have it. Our concept of security is inward-looking.' For the time being that conviction prevails, and has been reaffirmed by Thailand's Prime Minister General Prem Tinasulandonda among others. He said in October 1980 that the member states of ASEAN had come to realise the significance of depending on and supporting each other for their survival. Over five years later survival is not the issue, and the degree of military support desired and available remains limited. More-over, ASEAN states still look outside the walls of the Association for countervailing capability. Continuing defence relationships obtain between Thailand and the Philippines on the one hand, and the United States on the other, while Malaysia and Singapore retain an active interest in the Five-Power Defence Agreement

with Britain, Australia and New Zealand. Brunei, ASEAN's new
recruit, continues to play host to a battalion of Gurkha Rifles.

The prevailing view within ASEAN for the time being is that
its condition in terms of common threat and capability would
not justify transformation beyond its present political role.
Indeed, such transformation could well serve to undermine its
actual diplomatic strength if formal military cooperation proved
to be less than credible.

ASEAN has made substantial progress in regional cooperation
since 1967, in part because its member governments have always
held a realistic view about the appropriate pace of its evolution.
They appreciate not only the advantages of limited *ad hoc* military
cooperation, but also the evident disadvantages which could
follow from premature alliance formation. The Association may
in time evolve into more than a quasi-alliance; but the underlying
conditions for such a qualitative change in nature and role have
not been established and may never be so.

ASEAN remains essentially a diplomatic community conscious
of the limits to economic cooperation and of its relative military
weakness. It may be argued that diplomatic strength cannot
be sustained without an underpinning measure of economic
cooperation and of military capability. Such a judgement may
be proven correct one day. However, any attempt to give ASEAN
a collective military dimension would not necessarily serve the
ability of the Association to sustain that unity of purpose and
diplomatic concord which has distinguished its response to
conflict in Indochina. Correspondingly, economic cooperation
has also to take account of state interests.

CONCLUSION

ASEAN has evolved from its origins as an instrument for regional
reconciliation and internal political consolidation into a viable
structure for political and bureaucratic consultation, and also
for external bargaining. Its ability to sustain a unity of political
purpose since the onset of the third Indochina war would
suggest that it has also attained the status of a diplomatic
community. But the basic strategic concordance of its members
has been over internal security. Yet, in the absence of a true
unity of external strategic purpose it has been obliged to confront

security issues which are intrinsically divisive. Its ability to continue to manage this inner tension will determine the future promise of a regional partnership that has been a notable success by international standards.

11 Trade and Asian Pacific Nations

LOUIS TURNER

It would be difficult to be dull about this topic. On the one hand, Japan and 'the Gang of Four' (South Korea, Taiwan, Singapore and Hong Kong) have been vastly successful in manufactured trade. On the other hand, the success of the East Asians rests on a very fragile basis, in that these countries are very import-dependent for their energy. Finally, in the background, there is China, which could be emerging as a major source of manufactured exports in its own right.

MANUFACTURED TRADE

I will not cite a great many statistics, but we are basically dealing with three sets of countries in the region. First, there is Japan, which was becoming a significant exporter of textiles as early as the 1930s. Second, there are the four smaller East Asian 'miracle' economies, which began making their impact in the 1960s and 1970s. Finally, there is a group of other countries in the region, such as the Philippines, Thailand and Malaysia, which are now just starting to become significant exporters of manufactured goods themselves. From Table 1, it is possible to see that Japan's exports are about half those of the United States; that the exports from South Korea, etc., are about one-fifth of Japanese levels; and that Malaysia, Thailand and the Philippines each export between one third and one half of what Korea or Singapore have already achieved.

As befits the fact that these economies are all at different levels of development, the pattern of each group of countries varies in

132

TABLE 1   *The Leading Asian Exporters: 1981*

	Exports (US $ billion)	Share of manufactured goods in total exports (percentage in 1981)
(United States)	233.7	68.6
Japan	152.0	96.6
Hong Kong	21.7	92.3
China	21.6	n.a.
South Korea	21.2	93 *(1978)*
Singapore	21.0	49.0
Malaysia	11.2	27.8 *(1980)*
India	8.1	58 *(1977)*
Thailand	6.9	62 *(1978)*
Philippines	5.7	65 *(1978)*
Pakistan	2.9	51.3

SOURCE   *Yearbook of International Trade Statistics.*

terms of the kind of products which they export. Japan has already been through the textile era, and has been increasingly moving beyond basic manufacturing industries such as steel and shipbuilding. Today, the largest sector of Japanese exports is 'machinery and equipment', which includes everything from ships to automobiles, televisions and office machines. The proportional importance of this sector has been growing, in that it made up one half of Japanese exports in 1974, but almost two thirds of them by 1978.

The newly industrialising countries (Korea, Hong Kong) are still fairly heavily dependent on the textiles and clothing sector. However, they are moving fast into light electronics, such as calculators, television games and peripheral computer equipment. Countries like Korea and Taiwan have gone further and are involved in heavy industries such as steel, automobiles and petrochemicals. This is not to say that they are universally successful, for the Koreans have got themselves badly over-extended in such sectors and are having to pull in their horns. But, in general, the picture is of economies quite rapidly diversifying away from textiles and clothing.

The next generation of countries (Malaysia etc.) are more heavily dependent on textiles, but there is an opening for them to exploit as the wage levels of economies like that of Hong Kong and Taiwan move ever upwards. So Thailand is making black and white televisions, following some 10 years behind countries like Taiwan and South Korea.

These products are primarily for export outside the region. In the case of the Japanese machinery sector, almost one third of exports go to North America (primarily the United States), and one fifth to Western Europe (primarily the European Communities). Roughly, only one third of Japan's machinery exports go to Asia, and a part of this is to West Asia – that is, the Middle East.

The rapid success of such economies needs some explanation, despite the fact that this lures me into the field of popular sociology. It does appear that these economies are linked by the common strand of the Confucian tradition, which stresses the required benevolence of leaders, while demanding unquestioning obedience on the part of the led. Again, the Confucian tradition places quite high emphasis on education. So what we see in the region is a series of economies which, with the exception of Hong Kong, are led by governments which are more or less following the Japanese route to success. It would be foolish to deny that the state directs most of these economies, and that it can call on subservient labour forces and a degree of labour peace generally not seen in the West.

However, it is essential to point out that the success of these economies does not just rest on cheap labour – after all, there are plenty of other poor countries in the Third World which have not succeeded in taking off so fast. Instead, what one is seeing is the rapid trading up of the industrial skills of each of these countries. To take one small example, it is instructive to think about Japan's entry into colour televisions. Ten or fifteen years ago, Japan was technically behind the best practices of the West – though the Japanese authorities had, in the 1950s, identified consumer electronics as a sector in which the country should be established. In the early 1970s, the Japanese manufacturers got a jump on their Western competitors by realising the

12 The Balance of Power and Regional Order

MICHAEL LEIFER

East Asia has enjoyed a mixed place in the priorities of the major external powers. Yet as a region it is of abiding importance to their global considerations because its resident states, if one takes necessary account of America's military presence, comprise virtually the hierarchy of the international political system.

At one juncture, East Asia served as the military locus of the Cold War and in consequence the United States became engaged in a protracted involvement sustained by an obsession with the design of China and attendant problems of international credibility. East Asia is no longer affected by the same priorities of America's containment policy. Indeed, it has long ceased to be a major theatre of global conflict. In the wake of Sino-American *rapprochement* and the end of the second Indochina war, a new pattern of international alignments was formed which cut across a once accepted conventional structure of ideological affinities. And although East Asia has remained a geographic junction of contending interests, it has become a region where the balance of competitive advantage between global and local adversaries is not decisively weighted. In other words, it is not a region where any one state with client support is in a position to exercise a dominating influence. The rationale for America's protracted involvement in East Asia was to contain the prospect of an international communist domination exercised through the expansionist vehicle of the People's Republic of China. In effect, during the initial practice of this policy it was the United States which was the dominant power in East Asia and it may be argued that it was through the obsessive application of containment policy that such dominance was undermined.

143

Accommodation with China constituted a clear repudiation of the premise of containment in East Asia if it did not deal with the problem of international credibility which had arisen as a direct consequence of military intervention in Indochina. America's military failure in East Asia coincided with the rise of Soviet military power and its visible extension to Asia in naval form and also an intensity in Sino-Soviet antagonism which served to revise the regional and global pattern of alignments. Moreover, this revision of alignments also incorporated Japan so that by the end of the 1970s, it appeared as if a new structure of strategic relationships was in the process of consolidation.

Although the Soviet Union, despite its military expansion in East Asia, has remained very much the outside major power, the pattern of countervailing alignments has not hardened in the way some had anticipated. For example, although there have been practical understandings reached between the Chinese and American governments, the relationship has come to be seen to be based more on an interdependence of interests and their managed coincidence rather than on any special sense of convergence in strategic terms. A better sense of strategic understanding has developed between the United States and Japan served by the compatability of temperament of heads of government. America's sense of priorities has been governed by assessments of economic strength and of the political disutility of crudely playing the anti-Soviet card.

THE PATTERN OF STRATEGIC RELATIONSHIPS

If it is misleading to refer to a new structure of strategic relationships, the revised pattern of association has been sustained. For example, since their failure to come to terms over a peace treaty in the late 1970s concurrent with the conclusion of a Sino-Japanese treaty, Soviet–Japanese relations have been at a low ebb held down by the abiding obstacle of the northern territories. Moreover, the bilateral relationship has never been assisted by the intimidating tone of Soviet approaches; nor was it by the shooting down without apology of the Korean civil airliner with loss of Japanese lives.

In addition, China and the Soviet Union have changed the tone of their discourse since the early 1980s and have also taken a number of practical steps to co-exist but without expecting any return to the so-called golden age of their relationship. China, less fearful now of the Soviet Union, has continued doggedly to insist that its government fulfil three conditions before their relationship can be set on a truly new footing. Its government would seem to have made these conditions in the full knowledge that it would be most unlikely that the Soviet Union would comply in the cases of Afghanistan and Vietnam. The outcome of an early Soviet withdrawal from Afghanistan would lead to a major political reverse which the Soviet Union could not accept. And while in the case of Vietnam, the Soviet Union might be prepared to compromise the regional interests of its treaty partner for the global benefits of revising its relationship with China, there is no expectation in Moscow that China would be prepared to assume the kind of role that would make it worthwhile for the Soviet Union to risk a reverse for Vietnam in Kampuchea. As for the issue of the reduction of Soviet troop levels along the Sino-Soviet and Sino-Mongolian borders, this point of *impasse* reflects in part the underlying measure of mistrust which still informs the relationship between Moscow and Beijing, as well as the logistical perspective of the former.

Although it is possible to identify the pattern of major regional relationships, the term balance of power as a generalisation to explain that pattern is less than precise. As an indication of the condition of the relationship between states, it means the distribution of power. But the problems of introducing precision into an assessment of such a distribution are legion if only because quantitative indices are not sufficient on their own and do not lend themselves to necessary comparison. Balance of power as an actual policy of states has been clearer in terms of a common goal which has been to deny the emergence of any undue dominance or hegemony. Traditionally, the instrument of the balance has been war because in the last resort it was the only means available with which to preserve the independence of states. The advent of nuclear weapons, however, has transformed the classical positive relationship between war and policy. And in East Asia, three of the four principal powers possess such weapons if to a differing degree.

Of these four principal powers, Japan is ideologically non-nuclear and has never resorted to use of force since its surrender which marked the end of the Pacific War in 1945. Moreover, its military establishment, despite benefiting from an increasing government expenditure, has a great many shortcomings. Indeed, the prospect of its navy and air force being able to monitor and police home-island sea-lanes within a perimeter of 1000 nautical miles is not close at hand. The United States has been to war in East Asia in both Korea and Indochina and the legacy of that linked, bitter experience has yet to work its constraining effect out of the American body politic. Since military disengagement in 1973 and client *débâcle* in 1975, there have been a series of policy statements from Washington asserting a commitment to remaining a Pacific power. Underlying all such declarations, however, has been the guiding principle set in general terms by the Nixon Doctrine enunciated in 1969. In other words, United States governments have not indicated any intention of becoming directly involved again in any regional conflict in Asia, although they have been prepared to support allies and friends with military assistance and diplomatic backing.

The Soviet Union has enhanced its military position in East Asia including in Asiatic Russia and the disputed Northern islands. It engaged in border skirmishes with China in the late 1960s but apart from reinforcing its military position in East Asia especially since 1979 through access to facilities in Vietnam, it has not resorted to force as an act of policy even when China asserted its so-called right to punish Vietnam. The shooting down of the Korean civil airliner in September 1983 was in one sense characteristic of the Soviet security outlook but it was most probably a reactive miscalculation which certainly did not serve the interests of regional policy. An indication of a possible willingness to use force in East Asia was signalled, however, in April 1984 when joint land, sea and air exercises were conducted with Vietnam and a battalion of Soviet naval infantry (marines) were landed on a beach south of the port of Haiphong. These exercises were conducted concurrently with Sino-Vietnamese cross-border clashes and close to the visit by President Reagan to China. Undoubtedly, circumstances could arise when the Soviet Union might feel obliged to employ military sanctions against China should the People's Republic ever exercise its proclaimed right to teach Vietnam 'a second lesson'.

It is worthy of note that it is China which has made recurrent use of force in mixed circumstances, if in no way comparing with the scale employed in the past by the United States. Setting aside its use of force in South Asia or its ambivalent support for revolutionary movements in South-East Asia, China has used force in Korea in the early 1950s and then from the mid- to late 1950s against Taiwanese-held offshore islands as well as in border clashes with the Soviet Union. More recently, force has been used to occupy the Paracel Islands seized from the South Vietnamese in January 1974 and then in February 1979, China launched its so-called act of punishment against Vietnam in retaliation for the latter's invasion and occupation of Kampuchea. Since then, China has persistently sustained a state of military tension along its border with Vietnam in order to demonstrate its adamant refusal to become reconciled in the political identity of the government in Phnom Penh.

THE PROSPECT OF MILITARY CONFRONTATION

The grand issue of the balance in East Asia involving the structure of relationships between the major actors undoubtedly incorporates a military dimension but only a limited prospect of military confrontation. Military cooperation, however, has become of increasing importance and concurrently less controversial in the relationship between the United States and Japan. Since President Reagan's visit to China in April 1984, military cooperation in the form of the transfer of defence-related technology has proceeded apace. And for its part, the Soviet Union has sustained its degree of military readiness and made increasing use of facilties in Vietnam including a deployment there of MiG 23 interceptor aircraft in December 1984.

This measure of military shaping-up by the major powers is both a reflection of relationships and is intended also to influence them. It is not expected that armed confrontation will be a feature of this tilted set of quadrilateral relationships with the possible exception of its Sino-Soviet dimension. Before taking this matter any further to consider where resort to force might occur, it is important to assess the extent to which military power has influenced the balance of regional political influence. In such an assessment, Japan is ruled out because its government has not indicated any intention of seeking to advance its regional position through military means even if it has begun to shoulder an increasing measure of responsibility for self-defence.

The United States actually served to diminish its international standing and regional influence because of the unsuccessful protracted war which it fought in Indochina, although not beyond recovery. Indeed, there can be little doubt that the member governments of the Association of South-East Asian Nations (ASEAN) draw more than a measure of assurance from the continuing commitment of the United States to remain a Pacific power, expressed in military deployment. That deployment depends, of course, on access to an uninterrupted use of military facilities. Such facilities are at limited risk in Japan and Korea but have become vulnerable in the Philippines whose government has been in an advanced state of political decay. Ever since the assassination of opposition leader Benigno Aquino in August 1983, the political climate in the Philippines has become volatile and for opposition groups apart from the communists, America's tenure of military bases at Clark Field and Subic Bay has become a prime target. These bases are used for surface naval deployment as well as aerial reconnaissance and staging and have direct relevance to the Soviet military presence in Vietnam and importantly also for military operations in the Indian Ocean and the Gulf. Should radical political change force the United States to give up its bases in the Philippines, such a disengagement would do more than affect the balance of power in East Asia. Apart from the problem of finding alternative facilities of corresponding utility and the factor of additional sailing time involved in reacting to a crisis from any base east of the Philippines, the general political credibility of the United States would be bound to suffer in the process. In other words, while it is difficult to be precise about the political influence which the United States derives from its military presence in the Philippines, an enforced withdrawal of that presence would undoubtedly have adverse consequences for the exercise of such influence.

The Soviet Union has built up its military strength in East Asia, including the deployment of Backfire bombers and SS-20 missiles, primarily within territory subject to its direct control. There is no military presence on the territory of its North Korean treaty partner which has displayed a ferocious sense of independence if tilting for some time in the direction of China.

In the case of Vietnam, the Treaty of Friendship and Cooperation concluded in November 1978 marked a major progression in the relationship bearing in mind that such a treaty had never been required by the government in Hanoi during the entire course of the bitter military confrontation with the United States. In return for a commitment to Vietnam expressed in material and military assistance, the Soviet Union has been permitted to use military facilities in Da Nang and Cam Ranh Bay which, if not bases in the full sense, have extended the operational reach of its Pacific Fleet and have enabled it also up to a point to escape the constraints imposed by the maritime narrows around Japan. In addition, the Soviet Union has been able to develop its technical and military training presence in both Laos and Kampuchea which serves as an acknowledgement of Vietnamese weakness.

Soviet influence with Vietnam is a function of a dependent relationship but it does not extend to political control. The Vietnamese are capable of being quite as assertively independent as their North Korean counterparts. They conduct their relations with the Soviet Union on the basis of the conviction that the government in Moscow has a socialist duty to assist its fraternal partner. The problem for the Soviet Union in its relationship with Vietnam is that any advantages which accrue arise from a commitment to Vietnamese priorities. Apart from the obstacle which such a commitment places in the way of improving relations with China, it has also obstructed the development of rather more fruitful relations with the states of ASEAN. Moreover, the style of Soviet diplomacy and the crude attempts at espionage by its agents have not exactly made friends, while the tribulations of its economy have long discredited it as a model for developing East Asian states. The Soviet Union enjoys a grudging respect in East Asia on account of its disposal of considerable firepower which it deploys at a distance as a Superpower. But apart from an important but also uneasy relationship with Vietnam, the government in Moscow has not been able to convert such power into significant political influence in its relationships either with the major or minor regional actors.

The People's Republic of China is, of course, only a regional power despite its international standing. It has been willing to resort to force to cope with conflicts within its limited military reach. Influence, however, has come primarily from a sense of potential based on size, population and style. China casts a shadow over East Asia as an object of perplexity and wonder. In South-East Asia, for example, China both repels and attracts. It insists on dual standards of international conduct in enjoying diplomatic relations with regional governments while reserving the right to proffer, at least, moral support for revolutionary movements in the region which challenge the legitimacy of those same governments. In addition, the presence of sizeable and economically influential Chinese communities in South-East Asia serves as a point of continuing friction to the extent that the charge has been made recurrently that these communities constitute trojan horses to be manipulated at China's behest. China's actual use of force has produced mixed dividends. The claim to have taught Vietnam a lesson has produced a determined sense of resistance in Hanoi, while in Bangkok, China's willingness to use force has given the Thai government sufficient confidence to challenge Vietnam's occupation. Within the rest of ASEAN, corresponding mixed feelings have been expressed. For example, in Jakarta where China is viewed as a long-term threat, its willingness to use force to resolve conflicts to its own advantage is not seen to augur well for further relations.

The relationship between military strength and political influence is not all one way. Moreover, in the case of the major powers in East Asia, force has been used only to a limited extent in any decisive sense. Decisive use of force has been employed more by regional states and revolutionary movements. However, in attempting to make any general assessment of comparative political advantage arising from military position, then it must be said that the balance has moved away from the United States but not in any fundamental sense. Its principal adversary the Soviet Union has asserted a position which it never enjoyed at the height of the Cold War. Nonetheless in terms of economic capacity and facility for military regeneration as well as regional access and pattern of regional alignments, there can be little doubt that despite evident advances and the fact of strategic parity, the Soviet Union enjoys a position of lesser advantage in East Asia.

Within East Asia, there obtains a distribution of power that has changed significantly over the past four decades but not out of all recognition. Part of the key to continuity and change has been China's adversary relationships which because of its geopolitical position and their nature have given conflict in East Asia a global significance. Such a perspective arose initially when China was perceived in Washington as the vehicle for an expansionist international communism which the United States was duty bound to contain. Correspondingly, although China's adversary relationships have been radically reversed, the global significance of East Asian conflicts has been sustained while the change in the pattern of alignments has certainly compensated for American military failure and rising Soviet military strength.

The contest for the balance in East Asia expressed in terms of acts of policy in contention and cooperation has taken the general form of political manoeuvering to revise or sustain that pattern of alignments which took shape from the early 1970s. For example, the Soviet Union would like to be able to promote a greater distance in the relationship between China and the United States and ideally to revise to advantage its own relationship with Japan. In a sense this is what the Soviet Union would prefer as the basis for a system of regional order, that is, a structure of regional relationships that are widely accepted and serve its special interests at the same time. Such a system of regional order if preferable from Moscow's point of view is certainly not acceptable in balance of power terms among the other major states. Indeed the interacting network of global and regional relationships militates against the notion of regional order conceived in such terms because the requisite bases of common understanding necessary to underpin it do not exist. Moreover, the prevailing pattern of competition which is subversive of regional order does not seem likely to change in any significant way. American–Soviet relations which have regional expression are set by global considerations and whatever measure of accommodation might be reached over arms control, for example, it is most doubtful if there will be any early change of substance in their managed antagonism. Correspondingly, as long as China remains set on its current course of modernisation and inclines to the United States in terms of a clear priority of threats, there is little chance of any fundamental revision in relations with the Soviet Union. Indeed, the Chinese government makes sure of maintaining a strong political distance by insisting on its three virtually non-negotiable preconditions. Soviet–Japanese relations seem to be set in an even more rigid mould.

It is possible to argue that the general pattern of the regional balance in East Asia in terms of distribution of power embodies a measure of stability from a sense of prudence. But it is not the same as a viable regional order which requires more than just a rudimentary code of inter-state conduct. It requires also the existence of a set of shared assumptions about the interrelationships among resident and external states. Moreover, in East Asia there are certain issues of contention which have the potential to disturb that measure of stability that comes from a sense of prudence and not from any commitment to regional order. A prime example is Korea which is not at war; but neither is it at peace.

The major powers including China have displayed an evident interest in not disturbing the *status quo* in the peninsula but there are important competitive factors at work, not least in Sino-Soviet relations. The burgeoning economic success of South Korea, relative to the North, together with its notable achievement in international legitimacy by securing Seoul as the site for the 1986 Asian Games and the 1988 Olympic Games, has generated internal tensions within the government in Pyongyang. That government has been caught up in the management of dynastic succession as well as overwhelmed by frustration at not being able to realise its long standing claim to be the legitimate authority in the whole of a divided country. The revival of some kind of dialogue, if chequered, between North and South, reflects the changing balance of advantage between Seoul and Pyongyang but does not exclude the prospect of resort to force made dramatically apparent by the bombing of the Martyrs' Mausoleum in Rangoon in October 1983 which cost the lives of four South Korean cabinet ministers. The major actors in the region have no interest in such a course of action. Indeed, between China, Japan and the United States there has developed an informal consensus to which the Soviet Union is tacitly joined because it cannot calculate the consequences of another Korean War.

If Korea represents a dormant conflict but of volcanic potential, the struggle for Kampuchea has both a regional and global significance; it has engaged external interests with the effect of sustaining a military and diplomatic stalemate for which the burden of costs seems to be acceptable to all sides for the time being. The root cause of this conflict is Sino-Vietnamese antagonism. Its effect has been to produce political polarisation within South-East Asia and contention among the major powers on the same basis as the prevailing pattern of regional alignments. The issue in question is that of the local balance; namely, whether or not Vietnam is to be the dominant power in Indochina. In this matter, the states of ASEAN, augmented by the admission of Brunei in January 1984, have become deeply engaged but not in conventional balance of power terms. They do not constitute an alliance; nor an informal centre of military strength. The prime asset of the Association is its role as a diplomatic community and as such it acts collectively to keep the issue of Kampuchea alive through employing regional credentials, which have served it in such good stead to deny legitimacy to that government conveyed into Phnom Penh in the saddle bags of the Vietnamese Army. In consequence, it has been caught up in a wider structure of conflict which in its interplay obstructs ASEAN's own ideal design for regional order, that is a zone of peace, freedom and neutrality. Within this structure, it has been China which has been the principal mover in promoting a strategy of attrition designed to place breaking strain on society and government in Vietnam. In this exercise, it has engaged in punitive military action and has also reserved the right to teach Vietnam 'a second lesson'. Any such enterprise would risk Soviet retaliation but, so far, China has conducted its coercive diplomacy up to the brink and not beyond. Nonetheless, this is an evident danger of escalation of conflict which could have a greater destabilising effect regionally. Correspondingly, regional instability could be aggravated should Vietnam decide that the only way to eliminate all forms of Khmer resistance to its political design in Kampuchea would be to strike deep into Thailand to eliminate active sanctuaries.

Other outstanding regional issues of contention have either been settled or temporarily set aside. For example, the reversion of Hong Kong to China in July 1997 would seem to be a *fait accompli* if the supporting Anglo-Chinese agreement is remarkable for the public commitment of the government in Beijing. Moreover, the issue of Taiwan, still high on China's international agenda, has been managed as a source of friction in Sino-American relations, while its link with the Hong Kong agreement has served to control the fundamental conflict over the reunification of China. Correspondingly, other conflicts of potential such as those over competing claims for jurisdiction in the South China Sea have been suspended by contending regional states because of the high priority given to the Kampuchean issue. China and Vietnam have not wished to alienate any ASEAN states over this issue, for the time being.

Dormant, actual and potential conflicts in East Asia have been contained within manageable bounds and within a framework of constraint imposed by the sense of prudence of the major powers. The general balance in East Asia is influenced by this sense of prudence which up to a point informs the dominant relationships between the Soviet Union on the one hand and China, the United States and Japan on the other. But those relationships are beset also by a competitive edge which makes the notion of regional order an inappropriate point of reference. If East Asia is not the focus of intense Superpower competition, it is also not a region of Superpower neglect, while China and Japan have obvious intrinsic interests to protect. The balance of power that exists in terms of a condition is reflected in a competitive pattern of regional alignments. It is a pattern which is more acceptable for the time being to the United States, China and Japan than to the Soviet Union. Accordingly its revision or managed confirmation constitute contending alternatives but to be confronted primarily in political terms because prudence constrains the use of military means traditionally associated with the practice of the balance of power as a policy of states. The decisiveness of battle, of which Lord Beloff was right to remind us at the outset, is not part of the expectation of contending major parties in East Asia, except as between local proxies. But it is through them or because of them that a current tolerated equilibrium may be set in flux.

Index

Afghanistan, 8, 34, 145
Andropov, Yuri, 48, 49, 56
Aquino, Benigno, 148
Arkhipov, Ivan, 51
Association of South-East Asian
    Nations (ASEAN)
  attitude to United States military
      presence, 148
  membership of Brunei, 119, 153
  military cooperation, 128–30
  political evolution and role, 120–4,
      153
  response to conflict in Kampuchea,
      125–7, 153
Australia
  and Vietnam War, 87–8
  immigration policy, 91–2
  international economic relations,
      92–5
  relations with ASEAN, 90–1
  relations with Indonesia, 89
  relations with Vietnam, 90

Baldridge, Malcolm, 27
Beloff, Lord, 154
Bell, Coral, 84
Britain, interests in Asia, 13–14
Brown, Harold, 20
Brunei, 130
  membership of ASEAN, 119, 153
Brzezinski, Zbigniew, 21
Bull, Hedley, 91
Bush, George, 23
Butterfield, Fox, 65

Cambodia *see* Kampuchea
Cancun summit 1981, 22
Carter, Jimmy, 20, 26, 75, 113
Chalfont, Lord, 87
Chernenko, Konstantin, 48, 56, 114

China
  as a trading power, 138–9
  attitude to Taiwan, 21–3, 26–7
  Cultural Revolution, 63–5
  diplomatic relations with United
      States, 20
  economic difficulties, 66–9
  Hu Guang railway bonds, 25
  Joint Communiqué with United
      States on Taiwan 1982, 27
  nature of party system, 62–3
  relations with Hong Kong, 8–9
  relations with Soviet Union, 48–51
  relations with Vietnam, 100–6
  Shanghai Communiqué with
      United States 1972, 20
  Treaty of Peace and Friendship
      with Japan 1978, 35, 76
  use of force by, 146–7
Comecon, 56
Confucian tradition and economic
    growth, 134
Curzon, George, 8

Deng Xiaoping, 17, 18, 23, 25, 26,
    27, 28, 29, 63, 64, 70, 102
Diem, Ngo Dinh, 102
Dong, Pham Van, 126
Drake, Francis, 4
Dulles, John Foster, 19

Fang Yi, 102
Five Power Defence Agreement
    1971, 89, 129–30
Friedman, Milton, 10

Geneva Conference on Indochina
    1954, 100–1
Gorbachev, Mikhail, 48, 51, 56
Gurkha Rifles, 130

155

Haig, Alexander, 22
Hawke, Robert, 90
Hayden, William, 90
Heng Samrin, 106
Ho Chi Minh, 97, 102, 103, 104
Hoan, Hoang Van, 106
Holdridge, John, 23
Hong Kong, 9, 153
Hu Na, 24, 27
Hu Yaobang, 17
Hung Hua, 23

India, attitude to Soviet invasion of
     Afghanistan, 12–13
Indonesia
  annexation of East Timor, 89
  impact on ASEAN, 120–1
  relations with Australia, 89–90
  security outlook, 125–6, 150
Ito Masayoshi, 36

Japan
  defence expenditure, 80–1
  energy problems, 136
  international economic relations,
     77–9
  Northern Territories, 35, 76
  position on Afghanistan, 34–5
  relations with China, 75–6
  relations with Soviet Union, 53–4,
     76
  Ryūkyū Islands, 31
  Treaty of Mutual Security and
     Cooperation with United
     States 1960, 31, 74, 81
  Treaty of Peace and Friendship
     with China 1978, 35, 76
Jenkins, Roy, 88
Jiang Qing, 63, 70
Johnson, Lyndon Baines, 103

Kampuchea (Cambodia), 104–5, 152
  attitude of ASEAN to conflict over,
     152–3
  source of conflict over, 152–3
Kim Il Sung, 108, 110, 113
Kim Jong Il, 110
Kissinger, Henry, 104, 105

Korea, North
  economic problems, 110–11
  intentions towards South, 109–10,
     152
  position on re-unification, 112
  relations with Soviet Union, 54–5,
     113
Korea, South
  position on reunification, 112–13
  relations with Soviet Union, 114
  shooting down of civil airliner
     1983, 55, 144, 146

Laos, 99, 100, 105–6
Lawrence, T. E., 4
Le Duan, 103, 105
Lee Bum Suk, 114
Lee Kuan Yew, 13, 128
Lenin, V. I., 62
Luxembourg, Rosa, 62

Malacca and Singapore, Straits of,
     78, 137
Malaysia, 122, 126, 129
Mansfield, Mike, 35
Mao Zedong, 19, 20, 48, 53, 64, 102
Marx, Karl, 61, 62
Millar, T. B., 86
Miller, Bruce, 88
Mongolia, 46
Mosher, Stephen, 25

Nakasone Yasuhiro, 37, 38, 40–1, 73,
     78, 81, 82
Netherlands, 22
Nixon, Richard, 17, 19, 20, 27, 31,
     32, 75, 87, 104, 147

Ōhira Masayoshi, 30, 34
O'Neill, Thomas, 26–7

Papua New Guinea, 87, 90
Paracel Islands, 147
Park Chung Hee, 113
Peng Zhen, 27
Philippines, 126, 129, 148
  claim to Sabah, 121
  United States military bases in,
     148

Phoui Sananikone, 99
Pol Pot, 105
Prem Tinasulandonda, 129

Rangoon, bombing of Martyrs'
    Mausoleum 1983, 108, 152
Reagan, Ronald, 16, 17, 18, 21, 22,
    23, 24, 26, 28, 35, 39, 112, 114,
    115, 147
Rusk, Dean, 21

Satō Eisaku, 31
Schultz, George, 24, 25, 26
Singapore, 121, 128, 129
Smith, Adam, 10
Sohn Jae Shik, 112
Sonoda Sunao, 35
Soviet Union
    economic interests in Asia, 47–8
    invasion of Afghanistan, 46–7
    relations with China, 48–51, 144–
        5, 149
    relations with Japan, 53–4
    relations with Korea, 54–5
    relations with United States, 52–3
    relations with Vietnam, 46, 55–7,
        106, 145, 146, 149
    Treaty of Friendship and
        Cooperation with Vietnam
        1978, 149
    view of regional order, 151
Suharto, President, 123, 129
Sukarno, President, 84, 123
Suzuki Zenkō, 30, 34, 35–6, 81

Taiwan, 18, 21–3, 27, 104, 153
Tanaka Kakuei, 33, 37, 40
Thach, Nguyen Co, 90, 127
Thailand, 122, 128, 129, 150, 153
    security outlook, 125–6
Thanat Khoman, 122
Trotsky, Leon, 63

United States
    diplomatic relations with China,
        20
    Guam Doctrine 1969, 33, 87–8,
        146
    Joint Communiqué on China with
        Taiwan 1982, 27
    policy towards Indochina, 98–9
    relations with Soviet Union, 52–3
    Shanghai Communiqué with
        China 1972, 20
    Taiwan Relations Act 1979, 20, 21
    Treaty of Mutual Security and
        Cooperation with Japan 1960,
        31, 74, 81

Vietnam
    aims in Indochina, 104
    National Liberation Front of
        South, 103
    relations with China, 100–6
    relations with Soviet Union, 55–7,
        106, 145, 149
    Treaty of Friendship and
        Cooperation with Soviet
        Union 1978, 149
    United States policy towards, 98–
        100

Wei Guoqing, 100
Weinberger, Caspar, 24, 26, 27, 35,
    38
Whitlam, Gough, 87, 88, 91
Williamsburg summit 1983, 37, 40,
    79
Wu Xueqian, 24, 25

Zhang Aiping, 28
Zhang Chongquiao, 105
Zhao Ziyang, 18, 19, 22, 27, 28
Zhou Enlai, 20, 102, 103